BASIC TRAINING FOR
SPIRITUAL
INTELLIGENCE

BASIC TRAINING FOR
SPIRITUAL INTELLIGENCE

DEVELOP THE ART *of* THINKING LIKE GOD

KRIS VALLOTTON

Chosen

a division of Baker Publishing Group
Minneapolis, Minnesota

Published by Chosen Books
11400 Hampshire Avenue South
Bloomington, Minnesota 55438
www.chosenbooks.com

Chosen Books is a division of
Baker Publishing Group, Grand Rapids, Michigan

Printed in the United States of America

ISBN 978-0-8007-6183-7 (paperback)
ISBN 978-1-4934-3131-1 (ebook)

Cover design by LOOK Design Studio

21 22 23 24 25 26 27   7 6 5 4 3 2 1

Contents

Welcome to the Beginning of Spiritual Intelligence

You are about to embark on an incredible journey, an exploration that will have a profound impact on your life and the lives of those around you, as well as on future generations to come. Do you believe it?

I hope so, because this manual is written for you—a *His-story* maker disguised as an ordinary human who is living a normal life, but who is actually God's ambassador of heaven. You are someone who thinks like God. You access through the Holy Spirit the deeper dimensions of God's mind. You walk in power and know how to love the *hell* out of people.

If you don't identify with how I just described you, then I am here to tell you that you are on the precipice of discovering something wildly significant not only to your identity in God, but to how you approach the world. I say that with confidence, because I know that the more you experience your God-given spiritual capacity for brilliance—thinking beyond the confines of time and space, and thinking beyond the limits of human reasoning—the more profound an effect you will have in your sphere of influence.

My goal and prayer for you is that you greatly develop and increase your capacity for spiritual intelligence—or SQ—as you work through this manual and read my book *Spiritual Intelligence: The Art of Thinking Like God* (Chosen, 2020). I have based each module in this manual on a few chapters of the book, as noted in the module introductions. You will find it very helpful to have a copy of the book itself in hand as you work through this manual, so you can read the indicated chapters for more information. You will also find a *Spiritual Intelligence Quotient (SQ) Assessment* included in the book, which you might find hugely revealing to take as you begin this process of learning about and developing your spiritual intelligence.

May God hide you everywhere, from the palaces of royalty to the streets of obscurity, and may you transform everything your heart has the opportunity to touch.

Let the journey begin!

Much Grace,
Kris Vallotton

How to Approach This Study

This manual is divided into five modules. Each module is designed to engage your IQ (cognitive intelligence) and EQ (emotional intelligence), but also to go beyond both of these and develop your capacity for SQ (spiritual intelligence). Each lesson in the modules has been divided into three sections: "Access God's Thoughts and Ideas," "Renew Your Mind" and "Build New Neural Pathways." Here is a little bit about each section and what you will accomplish as you work through it.

"Access God's Thoughts and Ideas"

This section starts off each lesson with a biblical approach that will help you gain insight into the mind of Christ.

Throughout this section you will also find *Cognitive Connections*, which are questions designed to engage the mindsets you presently hold and allow you the opportunity to apply the new concepts you are learning.

"Renew Your Mind"

This section is the reflective portion of each lesson and will help you take what you are learning a step further. It will help you identify any thinking that is prohibiting your spiritual growth, and it will position you to partner with the Holy Spirit for healing, renewed vision and restored hope.

"Build New Neural Pathways"

This section contains practical activations that will help you build new neural pathways to spiritual intelligence.

You will partner with the Holy Spirit to step outside the boundaries of what is comfortable and access the mind of Christ. As you develop your SQ and learn how to apply it, you will begin to walk as God's "solutionary"—someone who helps bring His solutions to this world's challenges.

Here are some recommendations for maximizing your use of this manual as you develop the art of thinking like God:

- Resist the temptation to record logical answers as you work through the exercises in this manual. Instead,

intentionally allow the Holy Spirit to build and increase
your capacity for spiritual intelligence.

- Go at your own pace, but be consistent. It has been proven
  that when you practice specific behaviors consecutively,
  new and healthy neural pathways begin to form in your
  brain. This increases your capacity for spiritual intelligence and brings to light God's life-transforming thoughts
  and ideas.

- Use the tools provided—the *New Neural Pathfinder* and
  the *Engagement Tool*—which I will tell you more about
  in a moment and which you will find in the pages ahead.
  Also use the prompts and questions in the *Cognitive Connections*, reflections and activations throughout each section. I have specifically designed all these features with
  you in mind, and they are directly connected to developing
  your spiritual intelligence.

After you complete each module, the *Engagement Tool* will
help you organize the new spiritual insights you have discovered
within the lessons and will prompt you to create a plan of action. I
designed this tool to help you implement your newfound spiritual
intelligence in your daily life. You will find a separate *Engagement
Tool* included for you at the conclusion of every module.

The New
Neural Pathfinder Tool

Science has revealed that new neural pathways form in the brain when we repeat the same actions consecutively over time. These neural pathways, which we will learn more about in the lessons ahead, significantly impact our mental, physical and spiritual health. My goal throughout this study is to help you develop new neural pathways that will lead you directly to employing a greater level of spiritual intelligence in your life and daily activities. This *New Neural Pathfinder* tool is designed to give you a visual on how you are progressing toward that goal.

As you engage proactively in developing and using your SQ, use this tracking tool each time you complete any of the listed actions. Color in the box that corresponds to the action you've engaged in on any given day that you choose to keep track. Blank lines are provided so that in addition to the actions I have already listed, you can write in any other spiritually specific action that you would like to start implementing and tracking in your daily life.

Do not feel bound, however, to using this tool every day (although that would be ideal at the start). The numbers correspond to individual days, but not necessarily to days of the month, so feel free to go at your own pace! I do encourage you to use this tool consistently over a period of time—for example, while you are involved in this study. You can even do more than one *Pathfinder* sheet, and extras are provided for you at the back of this manual. This will help give you visual data on the SQ work you are doing, which often goes unseen because it is a work of the heart and mind.

The more areas you fill in on the *Pathfinder* as you go along, the more you will realize how far you are progressing in spiritual intelligence. If you fill in more than one sheet and each subsequent sheet has more sections colored in and more new things you are tracking, then you are making great progress! Seeing your SQ level expand on paper, in "living" color in your daily life, will encourage you as you grow in the art of thinking like God.

New Neural Pathfinder

a spiritual intelligence tracking tool

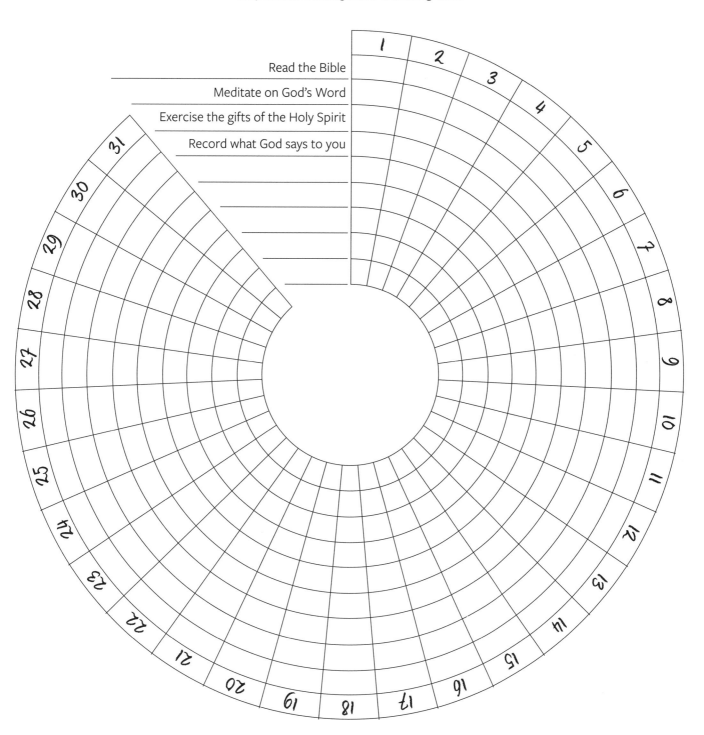

Read the Bible

Meditate on God's Word

Exercise the gifts of the Holy Spirit

Record what God says to you

Module 1

The Foundation of SQ

Like the famous astronaut Neil Armstrong, the first man ever to step foot on the moon, or like Jacques Cousteau, the great undersea explorer who searched the depths of the ocean, we are embarking on a journey to uncover the mysteries of the divine mind. One of the most famous ancient explorers in this regard was the great first-century apostle Paul. Although he was not the first human ever to experience the ability to think transcendently, he was one of the first ever to articulate his experience with a level of understanding that inspired many other explorers to join the journey.

Many people understand the concepts of IQ and EQ, and even AI (artificial intelligence), and realize that certain steps can be taken to heighten and strengthen these areas. Few people, however, have given much thought to the area of SQ. In fact, most are inexperienced in it. But if that includes you, that spiritual inexperience presents you with a fantastic opportunity to grow through this study! The invitation set before you today is to explore the nature of this whole new world of SQ with God, by way of the Holy Spirit.

Are you ready to forge ahead into the uncharted terrain of your spiritual mind? Before we begin this journey together, let's take a moment to do a preliminary self-check:

Based on your current perceptions, what do you think would be the single best measurable indicator that you are gaining spiritual intelligence?

_____

_____

_____

_____

Currently speaking, name any roadblock(s) you feel might prevent you from renewing the spirit of your mind.

_____

_____

_____

_____

Jesus says in John 14:26–28 that He will give us His peace and that the Father will also send us the Holy Spirit as our Counselor, who will guide us and teach us all things. Whatever roadblock(s) you listed, trust that the Holy Spirit is a wise navigator and that no perceived obstacle can stand in His way.

*For additional insights into module 1, read chapters 1–3 of my book *Spiritual Intelligence: The Art of Thinking Like God* (Chosen, 2020).

Lesson 1—Thinking Tri-Dimensionally

The apostle Paul inspired the expedition that you are about to set out on when he exhorted us as believers to "be renewed in the *spirit of your mind*" (Ephesians 4:23, emphasis added). On the surface, this seems like a simple exhortation to learn to think well, but on deeper examination, you will notice that Paul instructs us to renew not the lower dimensions of thinking, represented in modern times by IQ and/or EQ, but the "spirit of your mind." He was intentionally instructing us to give attention to a *specific* dimension of thinking—SQ. Let's jump in and glean what we can from the apostle Paul's insights about thinking tri-dimensionally.

Access God's Thoughts and Ideas

In 1 Corinthians 2:1–5, writing to a Greek church in the city of Corinth, Paul seeks to contrast the difference between the natural dimensions of wisdom and the divine wisdom available exclusively to believers:

> When I came to you, brethren, I did not come with superiority of speech or of wisdom, proclaiming to you the testimony of God. For I determined to know nothing among you except Jesus Christ, and Him crucified. I was with you in weakness and in fear and in much trembling, and my message and my preaching were not in persuasive words of wisdom, but in demonstration of the Spirit and of power, so that your faith would not rest on the wisdom of men, but on the power of God.

Underline in this passage what Paul experienced in the flesh. Circle what he experienced as he relied solely on the Holy Spirit's wisdom.

Paul makes it clear that he proactively restricted himself from accessing the "wisdom of man" so that he could demonstrate the superior benefits of God's divine power and wisdom. As I mentioned in chapter 1 of my book *Spiritual Intelligence*, at the age of thirteen and over the course of five years, Paul (then Saul) mastered Jewish history, the psalms and the works of the prophets, and he also learned to dissect the Scriptures. As a scholar, he then went on to become a lawyer and was likely on the fast track to becoming a member of the Jewish Supreme Court of 71 men who ruled over Jewish life and religion. With that context in mind, it is an incredible demonstration of faith when Paul informs the Corinthians that he has used restraint in accessing his own intelligence or the wisdom of man, and is resting solely on the wisdom of God, which he describes as "superior." This is also a sincere act of devotion to his call to serve God's people with God's ways and wisdom.

In 1 Corinthians 2:6–16, Paul goes on to instruct the Corinthians about how they, too, can think like God by accessing the mind of Christ:

> Yet we do speak wisdom among those who are mature; a wisdom, however, not of this age nor of the rulers of this age, who are passing away; but we speak God's wisdom in a mystery, the hidden wisdom which God predestined before the ages to our glory; the wisdom which none of the rulers of this age has understood; for if they had understood it they would not have crucified the Lord of glory; but just as it is written,
>
> > "Things which eye has not seen and ear has not heard,
> > And which have not entered the heart of man,
> > All that God has prepared for those who love Him."
>
> For to us God revealed them through the Spirit; for the Spirit searches all things, even the depths of God. For who among men knows the thoughts of a man except the spirit of the man which is in him? Even so the thoughts of God no one knows except the Spirit of God. Now we have received, not the spirit of the world, but the Spirit who is from God, so that we may know the things freely given to us by God, which things we also speak, not in words taught by human wisdom, but in those taught by the Spirit, combining spiritual thoughts with spiritual words.
>
> But a natural man does not accept the things of the Spirit of God, for they are foolishness to him; and he cannot understand them, because they are spiritually appraised. But he who is spiritual appraises all things, yet he himself is appraised by no one. For

who has known the mind of the LORD, that he will instruct Him? But we have the mind of Christ.

Notice how Paul begins his insights with the fact that we have access to a dimension of wisdom that is otherworldly and inaccessible to those who don't know God. Paul makes three observations about this divine wisdom:

1. *It's a mystery,* which is the Greek word *musterion*, meaning "secret doctrine." In fact, Paul goes on to tell the Corinthians, "Let a man regard us in this manner, as servants of Christ and *stewards* of the *mysteries* of God" (1 Corinthians 4:1, emphasis added).

2. *It's hidden from unbelievers, but available for believers.* King Solomon put it this way: "It is the glory of God to conceal a matter, but the glory of kings is to search out a matter" (Proverbs 25:2).

3. *It displays our glory.* In the days of Solomon, God's infinite wisdom was put on display for the Queen of Sheba, leaving her stunned and breathless. Likewise, the wisdom of God's Holy Spirit is to be demonstrated through us, His people, to the world around us. This divine demonstration not only brings glory to God; it also glorifies His people.

* *

*For additional insights, read the "Mind—Your Business" section in chapter 1 of my *Spiritual Intelligence* book. Also note that the definitions I provide of Greek and Hebrew words throughout this manual are taken from *Strong's Concordance*, which is readily available at various Bible-study sites online.

COGNITIVE CONNECTION

John 17:22 says, "The glory which You have given Me I have given to them, that they may be one, just as We are one." Highlight or circle the words *glory* and *one* in this verse, and then read it again.

Focus for a moment on this profound statement of Jesus. Sink into the truth that you and Christ are one. Allow the Holy Spirit to give you insight into what your life can look like when you are living in union with God. Record your thoughts in this anchor moment, as it will be foundational throughout this study:

_____

_____

_____

_____

_____

_____

It is important to understand that spiritual intelligence is not just accessing your own spirit or brain. Instead, it is connecting with God's Spirit, who is eternal, has all knowledge and wisdom, and knows the future. The Spirit has unfathomable experience with humankind and knows the heart of every person on the planet.

COGNITIVE CONNECTION

The brightest minds in the world today are still essentially relegated to IQ and EQ, virtually ignoring the deeper dimensions of SQ—our spiritual capacity for brilliance. Should you choose to disregard the infinite nature of your redeemed spirit-man through Christ, you will never think tri-dimensionally, using your IQ, EQ *and* SQ as God intended.

Having access to the mind of Christ gives you and me the ability to bring heaven's solutions to our daily lives, as well as to the global problems that face humanity. List one global challenge that you would like to gain spiritual intelligence about so you can help bring heaven's solutions to it.

_____

_____

Describe how this problem might be demonically influenced.

_____

_____

_____

How would the world be different if this situation were resolved?

_____

_____

_____

Renew Your Mind

You have just learned that as a believer, you have access to the mind of Christ. This means you are a steward of the intellectual properties of God that the Holy Spirit gives you access to. In what way do you see this reality affecting the following seven basic areas of your life?

Family relationships: _____

_____

_____

_____

Marriage relationship: _____

_____

_____

_____

Financial situation: _____

_____

_____

_____

Personal development: _____

_____

_____

Spiritual development: _____

_____

_____

Professional life: _____

_____

_____

Social life: _____

_____

_____

Where in your life do you see that the reality of SQ in operation would have the greatest immediate impact?

_____

_____

_____

_____

In what specific ways do you believe accessing God's wisdom will impact the overall master plan of your life? Why?

_____

_____

_____

_____

Build New Neural Pathways

God is going to give you divine wisdom that, if implemented, could radically change your life and potentially become a solution to help solve complex global challenges. Take some time with Jesus and thank Him for sharing with you His mind, wisdom and ways.

You have written down a global challenge that needs heavenly solutions. Take some time to access God's mind about it. Record here what the Holy Spirit shares with you and consider how to apply His wisdom to this challenge today. What is He showing you about how you personally can become part of a solution?

_____

_____

_____

_____

_____

_____

_____

_____

_____

_____

*Revisit the *New Neural Pathfinder* tool now to track the spiritual progress you made throughout this lesson.

Lesson 2—Renew the Spirit of Your Mind

The apostle Paul wrote, "Do not be conformed to this world, but be transformed by the renewing of your mind" (Romans 12:2). The critical question here is, *How* do we renew our minds so that we live in our divine advantage? We will be answering this over the next few lessons, but first let's gain some understanding about how our biological mind processes information.

Access God's Thoughts and Ideas

Are you ready for a crash course in neuroscience? I want to introduce you to three ways our brain processes information: *the principle of first mention, neural pathways* and *drawing conclusions while conserving energy.* Let's look at each of these a little more closely.

1. *The principle of first mention:* The first time you hear information about any subject, it becomes the *way* in which you view that topic from that point on. In other words, the information you receive first about something creates the lens by which you view that subject. Everything you hear or experience after the first exposure to that topic will be processed through the information you received first. The first-mention info in your brain creates a *truth lens* by which you measure and/or evaluate all other proceeding information concerning that theme. The principle of first mention creates a number of concerns, the primary concern being the unhealthy dynamic that takes place when first-mention info is wrong or inaccurate.

2. *Neural pathways:* Another fact I want to share with you comes from Dr. Caroline Leaf, a neuroscientist and the author of *Who Switched Off My Brain?* (Thomas Nelson, 2009). I learned from Dr. Leaf that our thoughts travel on brain highways called *neural pathways*, and that the more

> ### COGNITIVE CONNECTION
>
> Can you recall any belief or perception that the principle of first mention may have formed in you? Specifically, did you adopt any belief system because of it that might produce negative behavior that "feels right," but that you innately know is unfruitful?
>
> _____
>
> _____

> ### COGNITIVE CONNECTION
>
> Metaphorically speaking, visualize neural pathways being like the result when a hot marble is dropped through a block of cheese. The wider the highway becomes, the easier it is to repeat the same thought. You can see from my simple explanation how easy it is to create a superhighway of constructive or destructive mindsets.
>
> List one negative thought that seems to sabotage your progress repeatedly. What activity or circumstance triggers this repeated thought process in you? How has it sabotaged your success or growth in the past? What positive and/or scriptural thought can you practice replacing it with consistently?
>
> _____
>
> _____
>
> _____

we repeatedly have the same thought (positive or negative), the wider the physical highways or pathways for that thought to travel on become in our brain.

3. *Drawing conclusions while conserving energy:* One more fascinating nugget about how our brain processes information comes from Donald Miller, an American author and speaker and the CEO of StoryBrand. According to Miller's research, when our brains draw a conclusion about something, they use the least amount of energy to get to that conclusion. In other words, it is challenging to direct our minds to go a different route than what they are accustomed to.

Now that you have had a crash course in neuroscience, you see why it can be difficult to change our thought patterns. This is why it is vital for us to understand why Jesus gave us access to His thoughts by way of the Holy Spirit. The mind of Christ gives us access to divine wisdom, which is the ultimate spiritual intelligence. SQ therefore transforms our lives when we apply it.

Renew Your Mind

You have just learned about three neuroscientific facts that can make it difficult to change your mind. Yet the Holy Spirit has given you access to His mind, and He has also given you the ability to grow in your capacity for SQ—spiritual intelligence. On a scale of 0–4, how frequently has SQ influenced and shaped your life?

Perception Ruler

0	1	2	3	4
I am unaware of whether or not SQ is operating in my life.		SQ has only been an influence in certain circumstances.		SQ has influenced and shaped my life in every way.

Regardless of how you scored yourself, what opportunities do you see in your life to grow in spiritual intelligence with God?

_____

_____

_____

_____

Build New Neural Pathways

The Holy Spirit is the Genius of geniuses, the Scientist of scientists, the Doctor of doctors, the Engineer of engineers . . . you get the idea. He is the real definition of true brilliance.

Take a moment to ask the Holy Spirit to engage the divine imagination of God that He can give you access to. Ask Him to reveal the plans He has to prosper your life (see Jeremiah 29:11). You may get images, impressions, a knowing. . . .

Whatever way God communicates with you, remember that this is an opportunity to lean into God's understanding of your life, not rely on your biological brain's understanding of what you believe you can accomplish. Write here what He reveals to you:

_____

_____

_____

_____

_____

_____

_____

COGNITIVE CONNECTION

Think about the last time you were driving in your car. Did you take the shortest route to get from point A to point B? I propose that you did not take the shortest route, because the shortest route is actually as the crow flies. You probably followed the route your GPS suggested instead. To clarify Donald Miller's point about drawing conclusions and conserving energy, our minds will always take the quickest route, like a crow that flies the shortest, quickest route from one point to another. This is such a powerful image of _how_ we think and why it can be difficult to change our minds about life.

As you spend time with God this way, how do you see it increasing your capacity for spiritual intelligence?

_____

_____

_____

_____

_____

_____

_____

_____

_____

_____

_____

_____

_____

_____

*Revisit the *New Neural Pathfinder* tool now to track the spiritual progress you made throughout this lesson.

Module 1 | Lesson 3—Bulldozing New Neural Pathways

Know that with each lesson you complete about spiritual intelligence, you are actively building new neural pathways in your brain. Metaphorically speaking, you are hacking a fresh trail through the uninhabited jungle of your mind. The Word of God is like a machete in your hand, and the more often you abandon the six-lane freeway of destructive thinking and take the new walking trail of God-thoughts, the faster you will transform your mind. But the questions remain, *How* do you practically renew your mind, and *How* do you know when you have a renewed mind? Let's explore these questions and create some new pathways to spiritual intelligence at the same time.

Access God's Thoughts and Ideas

It is important to remember that the renewed mind does not just think differently; it also believes differently. In chapter 2 of my book *Spiritual Intelligence*, I differentiate between *high values* and *core values* this way:

- *High values* are the truths you hold in the greatest regard.
- *Core values* are what you truly believe—the way you actually see the world.

The example I use in the SQ book to illustrate this is that if you say, "God always takes care of me," but then you worry about His provision when your rent is due, your anxiety reveals this: Your *high value* is that God takes care of you, but your *core value* is that He really doesn't, or at least that He won't in this circumstance. Give a similar example you have witnessed of these two different values playing out in someone's life.

COGNITIVE CONNECTION

Reflect on a time when one of your high values clashed with a core value. Identify the two different values here:

High value: _____

_____

_____

Core value: _____

_____

_____

Core values are what you truly believe is true. This is why Jesus instructs us as believers to "take care how you listen" (Luke 8:18). *How* you listen is determined by your core values, which are the glasses your brain wears. In other words, it is not what you see, but *the way you see* it that affects your emotional state. Faith forms the lenses of your core-value glasses because it reveals what you actually believe deep down to be true. *Faith is the difference, the catalyst, between your high values and your core values.*

Jesus made a powerful statement that relates to this: "If you continue in My word, then you are truly disciples of Mine; and you will know the truth, and the truth will make you free" (John 8:31–32). The word *truth* in this passage is the Greek word *aletheia*, and it means "reality." In other words, the power of the transformed mind is that it rightly divides between fact and fiction, according to your faith in God.

Imagine that your rent or mortgage is due, and a thought comes to your mind that says, *No provision is coming; you're going to be homeless.* The renewed mind assigns that thought to the fiction room because the thought is opposed to the Word of God. The transformed mind accesses the "reality" compartment of the renewed mind to decide what to "believe" and adjusts your soul's emotional state accordingly. This aligns your reality with God's, as well as giving you access to heaven's solutions.

*For additional insights on these values and their interaction, read the "Core Values Versus High Values" section in chapter 2 of my *Spiritual Intelligence* book.

Now that you are actively engaging a renewed mind, let me introduce you to the guy in the Bible who exposed me to the reality of having a transformed mind. His name is Joshua, and I related some of his compelling story in *Spiritual Intelligence*. Joshua followed Moses, the most famous leader in the history of the world at the time. Moses spoke to God face-to-face, parted the Red Sea and did countless miracles, but he also left a vital, God-given task unfinished. After forty years, he was unable to lead God's people into the Promised Land. The unfinished task then fell to his servant Joshua. God Himself broke the news to Joshua, proclaiming, "Moses My servant is dead; now therefore arise, cross this Jordan, you and all this people, to the land which I am giving to them, to the sons of Israel" (Joshua 1:2).

I can only imagine the stress that must have fallen on Josh that day. His mentor was gone, the people were stressed out, and God was giving him an impossible mandate. Yet God shared a secret with Joshua that would ultimately be the key ingredient to his profound success. God exhorted Joshua several times to "be strong and courageous," and then He finished His exhortation with these final words: "This book of the law shall not depart from your mouth, but you shall meditate on it day and night, so that you may be careful to do according to all that is written in it; for then you will make your way prosperous, and then you will have success" (Joshua 1:8).

Notice that in effect, God told Joshua, "By meditating on My Word, you will make your way prosperous and have success!" Did you catch the "you will" part? God didn't say, "*I* will make you prosperous and successful." He said, "*You* will make your way prosperous, and *you* will have success."

A look at the Hebrew word *meditate* yields huge revelation into Joshua's success. The word *meditate* in this passage is the Hebrew word *hagah*, meaning "to growl and declare" (among a few other things). This Hebrew word is used in Isaiah 31:4: "For thus says the Lord to

---

COGNITIVE CONNECTION

Identify the lie(s) preventing the high value you identified from being your core value.

_____

_____

_____

_____

_____

_____

_____

_____

_____

_____

_____

_____

COGNITIVE CONNECTION

Underline what God told Joshua to do in Joshua 1:8 so that he would have success.

COGNITIVE CONNECTION

Write out Romans 12:2:

_____

_____

_____

_____

_____

_____

_____

_____

_____

_____

_____

_____

_____

_____

Remember, you may not feel as though you can change your life, but if you change your mind, God will transform your life. Take time in prayer to meditate on Romans 12:2.

me, 'As the lion or the young lion *growls* over his prey . . .'" (emphasis added). The English word *growls* is that Hebrew word *hagah*, translated as "meditate" in the book of Joshua. The point is that meditation in God is not sitting in a corner humming to ourselves; it is proactively bulldozing new neural pathways into our brains. This is God's formula for a renewed mind!

Meditating on the Word of God will determine what things your mind assigns to the fiction room and what things it assigns to the fact room. Meditation is therefore more than memorizing Scripture. It is making a proactive decision to believe God, to put truth above facts and to trust in His goodness in *your* life. Joshua-type meditation moves God's Word from memory to reality and changes your destiny.

Renew Your Mind

Much of what is being taught about the renewed mind today is behavior modification and not transformation. How do you know if you actually have a renewed mind? I have come up with the following eight symptoms that are often signs of a renewed mind. This is not a complete list from the broad spectrum of things that could indicate a renewed mind, but it's a good cheat sheet to help you assess where you are now.

Make an honest assessment of yourself in regard to each symptom, and choose a number on the following scale of 0–4: 0 = none; 1 = a little bit; 2 = at certain times; 3 = mostly; 4 = always.

1. You are full of hope.

   0 ——— 1 ——— 2 ——— 3 ——— 4

   What led you to pick this number?

   _____

   _____

2. The impossible seems reasonable.

   0 ——— 1 ——— 2 ——— 3 ——— 4

   What led you to pick this number?

   _____

   _____

3. You live in peace and you don't worry; your speculations are positive.

   0 ——— 1 ——— 2 ——— 3 ——— 4

   What led you to pick this number?

   _____

   _____

4. You like yourself and even rejoice in your weakness, knowing that when and where you are weak, God is strong.

   0 ——— 1 ——— 2 ——— 3 ——— 4

   What led you to pick this number?

   _____

   _____

5. You are quick to forgive, and you freely give others grace and mercy.

0 ———— 1 ———— 2 ———— 3 ———— 4

What led you to pick this number?

_____

_____

6. You are confident and thankful.

0 ———— 1 ———— 2 ———— 3 ———— 4

What led you to pick this number?

_____

_____

7. You believe in others and give them the benefit of the doubt.

0 ———— 1 ———— 2 ———— 3 ———— 4

What led you to pick this number?

_____

_____

8. You know how to think tri-dimensionally (IQ, EQ, SQ).

0 ———— 1 ———— 2 ———— 3 ———— 4

What led you to pick this number?

_____

_____

Build New Neural Pathways

God's one-liner to Joshua in Joshua 1:8 makes it clear and straight-forward: Meditate on His Word, and then do it!

Do you feel as if God has called you to something, but you have not taken the next step? Describe the last thing you feel God called you to.

_____

_____

_____

_____

Could the incongruity between one of your high values and one of your core values be keeping you from taking the next step? Identify that here. (For example, "My high value is that God has called me to heal the sick. My core value is that I struggle with believing people will be healed when I lay hands on them.")

High value: _____

Core value: _____

You can break the cycle of living below God's promises in your life by discovering the truth that will transform your high values into your core values. Write out any Scriptures, promises from God or prophetic words that will help you begin the journey of aligning your life to God's truth. (For example, "The Word of God says in Mark 16:17–18 that I will lay hands on the sick and they will recover. I also remember the day when that lady gave me a prophetic word that I would heal the sick.")

By doing this kind of exercise, you are building an arsenal that will destroy the lies operating in your life and build a new path to your destiny and purpose.

_____

_____

_____

_____

_____

_____

_____

_____

_____

*Revisit the *New Neural Pathfinder* tool now to track the spiritual progress you made throughout this lesson.

| **Lesson 4—Accessing Your Superpower: God's Thoughts in Real Time**

What if I told you that God is still empowering superheroes? What if I told you that you actually have a great advantage over the heroes we read about in the Old Testament, heroes like Daniel, Shadrach, Meshach and Abednego, among others? Crazy, right? *But true!*

Access God's Thoughts and Ideas

We talked in the previous lessons about renewing our minds and building neural pathways into new methods of thinking, both of which are formidable in transforming our personhood. Yet we develop God-given "superpowers" that are actually rooted in the "spirit of our mind" when we refuse to relegate problem solving only to our natural mind (IQ and EQ), and instead discern when to access God's thoughts in real time (SQ). Let's look at a biblical example that illustrates my point. I quoted this passage in the book as well, but let's read it again so we can discuss it further here:

> Now a certain woman of the wives of the sons of the prophets cried out to Elisha, "Your servant my husband is dead, and you know that your servant feared the LORD; and the creditor has come to take my two children to be his slaves." Elisha said to her, "What shall I do for you? Tell me, what do you have in the house?" And she said, "Your maidservant has nothing in the house except a jar of oil." Then he said, "Go, borrow vessels at large for yourself from all your neighbors, even empty vessels; do not get a few. And you shall go in and shut the door behind you and your sons, and pour out into all these vessels, and you shall set aside what is full." So she went from him and shut the door behind her and her sons; they were bringing the vessels to her and she poured. When the vessels were full, she said to her son, "Bring me another vessel." And he said to her, "There is not one vessel more." And the oil stopped. Then she came and told the man of God. And he said, "Go, sell the oil and pay your debt, and you and your sons can live on the rest."
>
> 2 Kings 4:1–7

This widow never would have needed a supernatural solution if she'd had natural provisions. Likewise, we often don't develop "the spirit of our minds" because we usually try to solve life's challenges with lower-level, natural thinking—thinking that can be based in biblical principles, but may not actually be Spirit led. In other words, Elisha could have told the woman in passing that God would supply her needs and could have then gone on his way. But he didn't; he took action in the moment. In chapter 2 of my book, we learned more about how to think biblically by meditating on God's Word, which helped make Joshua successful. Biblical thinking is life-transforming because it teaches us *how* God thinks. But the only way to know *what* God is thinking in real time is to have a connection through the Holy Spirit to God's mind. Let's dig a little deeper into the application of this. The apostle Paul wrote,

> For who among men knows the thoughts of a man except the spirit of the man which is in him? Even so the thoughts of God no one knows except the Spirit of God. Now we have received, not the spirit of the world, but the Spirit who is from God, so that we may know the things freely given to us by God, which things we also speak, not in words taught by human wisdom, but in those taught by the Spirit, combining spiritual thoughts with spiritual words.
>
> 1 Corinthians 2:11–13

Paul is pointing out that we have received God's Spirit, and we therefore have access to His thoughts. The key distinction here is that we are *not* just thinking *like* God; instead, we are thinking His actual thoughts planted in us by the Holy Spirit, knowing His mind in whatever situations we face, and mirroring His imagination about the solutions and outcomes in real time! This is our God-given superpower. At any time, in any circumstance, we can instantly access the mind of God about something, as the Holy Spirit gives us insight into it.

In order to pave new neural pathways to *divine* thinking, we will proactively have to discipline ourselves to forgo our initial rational conclusions in order to allow room for divine imagination to emerge. Furthermore, we will have to get comfortable with solutions that *sometimes* defy logic and reason (although not always) in order to embrace God's superior thinking.

As you engage your SQ and operate in divine wisdom, here are five things to remember:

1. Natural thinking will often challenge our ability to build neural pathways to divine thinking, because, metaphorically speaking, we have six-lane freeways already built into our lower levels of intelligence.

2. Oftentimes, God thinks outside the laws of physics since He lives in a superior reality. Many of His solutions therefore transcend the laws of nature, the facts and natural reason. It can be unnerving to wait on God, only to have Him give you a resolution that takes extreme faith and could cause you more trouble with people than the situation you are trying to resolve is causing.

3. Renewing our minds through biblical meditation so that we think like God is life-transforming. Renewing the spirit of our minds in such a way that we are mirroring God's thoughts concerning situations, circumstances, people or things, etc., is like the *Renewed Mind 2.0*.

4. Renewing the spirit of your mind is really about learning to hear the voice of God by allowing time for your spirit to build a friendship with the Holy Spirit and ultimately bond spirit-to-Spirit.

5. Much like any other relationship, building a friendship with the Holy Spirit takes time. There is simply no substitute for experience. We begin the process by asking the Holy Spirit what He thinks about various things throughout our day, and then we listen spirit-to-Spirit for His answers.

Renew Your Mind

Have you ever accessed God's thoughts in real time or experienced a supernatural solution like Elisha with the widow, the kind that required what felt like extreme faith? Briefly describe what happened.

_____

_____

_____

_____

_____

Paul says in 1 Corinthians 2:11–13 that the Holy Spirit teaches us, combining spiritual thoughts with spiritual words. In what way do you frequently experience the Holy Spirit teaching and speaking to you (visions, dreams, an audible voice, a sense of knowing, etc.)?

_____

_____

_____

_____

_____

Build New Neural Pathways

Work on building a friendship with the Holy Spirit by asking Him what He thinks about simply anything of your choosing. Think of something you would love to hear God's insight on regarding your life or relationships. Ask Him about it, with the intention of learning to listen spirit-to-Spirit. Make note here of how you discern His voice, the unique way He communicates with you and specifically what He says. Continually practice this throughout your day about different things to develop your bond with the Holy Spirit.

_____

_____

_____

_____

_____

_____

_____

_____

_____

_____

*Revisit the *New Neural Pathfinder* tool now to track the spiritual progress you made throughout this lesson.

Engagement Tool

The Top 4

List the top 4 spiritual insights you gained from this module, whether they came from the thoughts in the lessons, the *Cognitive Connection* exercises, the "Renew Your Mind" reflections or the "Build New Neural Pathways" activations.

1. _____

   _____

   _____

   _____

2. _____

   _____

   _____

   _____

3. _____

   _____

   _____

   _____

4. _____

   _____

   _____

   _____

Plan of Action

Create one action step based on the spiritual insights listed above that would demonstrate spiritual intelligence when you apply it to your daily life. Note that a good action step has a *who*, *what*, *how* and *when*. For example, if one of the spiritual insights I learned from this module is that God gives us supernatural solutions in real time, I would create an action step like this for myself: "As challenges present themselves in real time (*what* and *when*), I (*who*) will access the mind of Christ through prayer, gain God's wisdom and confidently act on or share the solutions with those people (*whom*) it pertains to (*how*)."

*Note that the *Spiritual Intelligence Quotient (SQ) Assessment* in my SQ book will give you many other specific action steps you can take to further develop, deepen and implement your SQ, based on your score once you take the test.

Module 2

The Art of Thinking Like God

It is important to remember that God is not human. His first language is not English, Spanish or German, nor is it any other human language that you or I might speak, although it is not uncommon for Him to speak to us in our language. Yet one of the most common ways the Spirit speaks to us is in a language I call "Spiritual Hieroglyphics." Although we most often associate hieroglyphics with Egypt, the word *hieroglyphics* is Greek. *Hiero* means "holy," and *glyphics* means "marks" or "writings," so the two together mean "holy writings."

To be clear, I am not saying that God was inspiring the Egyptian cave writings or anything remotely similar. I am using the word *hieroglyphics* as a way to illustrate how the Holy Spirit often speaks to us in picture form. What's even better is that you and I have been given the Holy Spirit, who relays the imaginative imagery of God's mind and helps us interpret the significant meanings behind this Spirit-filled communication. It is an awe-inspiring truth that God has equipped us to understand what He shows us about what He knows, and He also enables us to see what He sees in various people or situations.

All believers are equipped to interpret the languages God uses to speak to them. Are you ready to increase your receptivity to spiritual hieroglyphics? Before we start, let's take a moment to assess what you may have already experienced. God can speak to us through many visual experiences such as dreams when sleeping, visions when awake, or flashes of pictures or movie clips that play on the movie screen of our imaginations. Which of these visual experiences have you experienced so far, if any?

_____

_____

_____

If you have experienced some of these, circle how often God visually communicates with you in this way:

Frequently ———— Occasionally ———— Never

If you have had such an experience, have you also been able to receive the interpretation (for yourself or others) that comes along with God's visual communication with you?

_____

_____

_____

If you have never had such an experience, are you willing to open your heart and allow the Holy Spirit to speak to you in new ways? Trust the Holy Spirit in your journey. God is the one who created this often ignored and unexplored terrain of spiritual intelligence, so He will guide you through it. Yet He is not at all concerned about taking you and me outside our comfort zones as we develop our SQ.

*For additional insights into module 2, read chapters 4 and 5 of my book *Spiritual Intelligence.*

We have all seen the good, the bad and the ugly when it comes to people announcing things in the name of God. This has created a hesitation in some people about listening to the "voice" of God. Then the big question becomes, How do we actually cultivate a relationship with the God of the universe if we are afraid to hear from Him?

Access God's Thoughts and Ideas

What kind of Creator would design a creature like humans, with our level of capacity for communication, and then have no interaction with them—especially a Creator who calls Himself the Word of God? How could a God named the *Word* not talk to us? And if God is talking to us, then why are most people not hearing Him, or at least not understanding Him?

Consider Proverbs 25:2: "It is the glory of God to conceal a matter, but the glory of kings is to search out a matter." When it comes to communication between God and His people about different matters, what role do we play?

You have no doubt heard the saying that knowledge is power. Although God has placed us in a position of authority as His children, He does not want any of us to develop into tyrants. He therefore conceals His voice in such a way that it is only revealed to the humble and the hungry. That's a provoking thought, isn't it? But is it biblical?

We can learn more about this from the life of Joseph. He not only heard from God through dreams containing spiritual hieroglyphics, but he also, as many of us know, learned valuable lessons in humility.

Joseph had a dream, and when he told it to his brothers, they hated him even more. He said to them, "Please listen to this dream which I have had; for behold, we were binding sheaves in the field, and lo, my sheaf rose up and also stood erect; and behold, your sheaves gathered around and bowed down to my sheaf." Then his brothers said to him, "Are you actually going to reign over us? Or are you really going to rule over us?" So they hated him even more for his dreams and for his words.

Now he had still another dream, and related it to his brothers, and said, "Lo, I have had still another dream; and behold, the sun and the moon and eleven stars were bowing down to me." He related it to his father and to his brothers; and his father rebuked him and said to him, "What is this dream that you have had? Shall I and your mother and your brothers actually come to bow ourselves down before you to the ground?"

Genesis 37:5–10

Underline both of Joseph's dreams in the passage above. List the three spiritual hieroglyphics (pictures that communicate significant meaning) in the first dream:

1. _____

2. _____

3. _____

List the three spiritual hieroglyphics in the second dream:

1. _____

2. _____

3. _____

Joseph's dreams illustrate not only the hieroglyphic nature of the Holy Spirit's language, but also the fact that Joseph's family understood how to decipher that dialect. Of course, the bowing sheaves represented his brothers, and later the sun, moon and bowing stars signified his entire family honoring him. In case you are unfamiliar with the rest of the story, many years later Joseph became a ruler in Egypt, preceding a time of severe famine. He saved his family from destruction as they fled their country and came to Egypt to avoid starvation. Ultimately, his entire family bowed down to him in honor, just as the dreams had foretold.

As we learn to interpret the spiritual language of God, we must also grow to understand that we are accountable for what we know—meaning that the more clearly we understand the will of God, the greater our capacity is to rebel, sin or disobey Him. We can learn from Joseph. Notice that he acted without wisdom or humility in communicating to his family about his God-ordained future. This cost him severely, and he consequently spent many years of his life enslaved and imprisoned. Just as much as it is important to discern the multifaceted ways that God communicates with us, He also desires us to use wisdom and humility when we involve others in our lives and attempt to walk out the powerful promises He gives us.

Remember, to those who allow God's Spirit to live inside them, He gives the mind of Christ and His heart (reread 1 Corinthians 2:6–16). This does not remove our free will or speak of our character, but it does reveal God's will for us in varying degrees.

Renew Your Mind

As we discovered in Proverbs 25:2, God hides things for us, not from us. As honestly as possible on a scale of 0–4, evaluate how hungry and willing you currently are to seek understanding and discover the interpretation of spiritual matters, not only for yourself, but for others:

> **COGNITIVE CONNECTION**
>
> Have you ever had a dream with spiritual hieroglyphics in it, but you did not know how to discern the dialect God was communicating with you in? Write out your dream here and underline the hieroglyphics (images or symbols) that you didn't fully understand.
>
> _____
>
> _____
>
> _____
>
> _____
>
> _____
>
> _____
>
> If you have never experienced a dream like this, but you want to grow in this kind of spiritual "language," pause and ask the Lord to allow you to encounter Him tonight in your dreams.

0 ————— 1 ————— 2 ————— 3 ————— 4
Unwilling   Interested   Very willing

Process your hunger level. Write an honest confession when it comes to your hunger level and your willingness to grow in learning the hieroglyphics of the Holy Spirit. Know that God already sees your heart, so take this opportunity to process this further with Him. Expose your hopes, concerns or questions to Him when it comes to growing in your discernment and your interpretation of the language He uses to communicate with you.

Build New Neural Pathways

Using your dream and the spiritual hieroglyphics you listed in the previous *Cognitive Connection*, take a moment with the Holy Spirit and ask Him to help you interpret the unknown hieroglyphics from your dream. If you didn't have a dream to record, but you have a vision or some type of other imagery you feel God has given you, use that to complete this activation. Or you can ask someone else to share one of his or her dreams with you that needs interpreting.

Tip: Take each "hieroglyphic" one at a time and ask the Holy Spirit to give you the interpretation. Write out the interpretations you receive. After you complete this, look at the dream as a whole and record what you believe God wants to reveal to you (or to the person who shared a dream with you).

*Revisit the *New Neural Pathfinder* tool now to track the spiritual progress you made throughout this lesson.

Lesson 2—Receiving and Interpreting the Secret Message
Lesson 2—Receiving and Interpreting the Secret Message

It is clear throughout Scripture that the interpretation of visions and dreams is somewhat a spiritual skill that is at least partially learned through experience and training. In fact, this skill was often passed down in Bible days from generation to generation, as it was through Abraham's legacy. This was demonstrated in Abraham, his son Isaac, his grandson Jacob and his great-grandson Joseph, as well as in all Joseph's brothers. These descendants of Abraham were all guided by dreams and visions that they understood.

As you develop the art of thinking like God, you will come to understand that the level of our spiritual intelligence is determined by the depth of our relationship with our "Spirit Guide," who is the Holy Spirit. The Holy Spirit has been assigned to guide us into all truth (see John 16:13).

Access God's Thoughts and Ideas

The more experience you gain in the art of thinking like God, the more you will increase your spiritual intelligence—your SQ—and the more clearly you will understand His voice and be able to act on what He is telling you. Let's begin warming up your SQ muscles by considering the following four keys for understanding the languages of the Spirit.

1. *Cultivate a high value for hearing God.* It is important that you have a high value for hearing God so that you pay close attention to the spiritual "episodes" you have. The entire spirit world operates by faith, which is demonstrated through valuing the gift God has given you.

2. *Faith in God is spelled R-I-S-K.* You must be willing to take risks to see the Spirit move in power through you. These risks should not harm others, however, so it's probably wise to start out by cultivating a level of calculated risk at which you can learn and grow in the Spirit. I found

COGNITIVE CONNECTION

In Module 1 | Lesson 3 we discussed the difference between high values and core values. In the case of receiving and interpreting things from God, some people may have a high value for hearing His voice, yet their core value is that they do not believe He will speak to them, or they think they cannot hear Him. Write out the high value you have for hearing God's voice.

High value: _____

Currently speaking, do you have any core value that might clash with your high value for hearing God's voice? If so, what is it?

Core value: _____

COGNITIVE CONNECTION

List three questions (start with three) you have that are specifically related to how to hear God's voice.

1. _____

2. _____

3. _____

Taking ownership of your growth, how do you plan to seek understanding about the questions you wrote down?

_____

_____

_____

_____

_____

_____

that one of the best ways to begin living this way in the Spirit is to experiment with people with whom I already have a relationship by asking them a lot of "prophetic" questions. It's important to note here that the less experience you have, the more questions you should ask *before* making any kind of confident prophetic declaration to someone.

3. *Look for patterns.* Pay attention to the prophetic interpretations that you get right, because a language pattern will begin to emerge from these positive experiences. A clear understanding of God's personal dialect (the way He speaks to you) will materialize in your life, and soon you will be reading His pictorial language accurately.

4. *Don't fill in the gaps.* Sometimes it helps to describe a vision or image to the people you are ministering to and ask them what it means to them. Often, God will speak to you in *their* personal dialect instead of *yours.* For example, God gave me a certain number from the time I was young. It is God's secret code for me. Whenever someone uses that specific number, I know that person is hearing from God for

me. The number is meaningless to others, but to me it means God is saying, *Pay close attention to what this person tells you, as I am speaking to you through him [or her]*.

Renew Your Mind

Read Matthew 18:19–20. What does Jesus say He will do for a community in unity?

_____

I believe surrounding yourself with support and accountability is vital in developing a healthy SQ. One way I do that is by cultivating a prophetic community around me. I don't look for rock stars, simply individuals who have a hunger to grow in the mind of Christ and walk with the Holy Spirit. I highly encourage you to proactively surround yourself with people who are hungry for all of God, instead of waiting for them to come to you.

Name two to three people whom you feel comfortable growing spiritually with and exercising your SQ muscles on. Note that they should demonstrate some level of SQ themselves, or at least have a hunger to develop their spiritual intelligence further.

1. _____

2. _____

3. _____

COGNITIVE CONNECTION

Name at least one form of communication that you often experience from God.

_____

_____

What's usually happening around you when you are discerning God's voice? Are you always alone? Are you always with other people? Are you always asleep, or most often awake when you hear from God? Describe any other noticeable patterns that often take place when you are discerning God's voice.

_____

_____

_____

_____

_____

_____

_____

_____

_____

_____

COGNITIVE CONNECTION

Do you have a secret code from God, a certain sign no one else knows about that you discern is God's way of telling you to pay attention because He is speaking? What is it? (If you don't have one right now, that's okay.)

_____

_____

_____

If you have not yet identified a certain sign, take time to think about the patterns you listed a moment ago. Looking at these patterns, is there anything you can discover that you feel is a signal God has used through other people or things to reveal Himself to you?

_____

_____

_____

_____

This week, reach out to the names you listed and tell these people about the journey you are on. Share with them the three questions you listed that are specifically related to how to hear God's voice, and explain that you are looking to gain experiential insight from the Holy Spirit on those questions. Ask each of them if he or she would be willing to be a supportive friend on your journey of learning as you take risks and develop your SQ. Clearly articulate what you need from them, whether it is listening to you process your development, taking risks with you or praying for you. (More moments are ahead in this study when you will want to lean on these individuals, so involving them now will be beneficial for your growth.)

Build New Neural Pathways

Using the four keys we just looked at for understanding God's spiritual language, complete the following exercise.

1. *Cultivate a high value for hearing God.* Ask the Holy Spirit to give you a specific picture for one of the individuals you listed above. You may see a single image or multiple things, or you may experience a mini-movie or vision in your imagination. Write it down. Ask the Holy Spirit to give you the interpretation. Make a note of that, too.

   _____

   _____

   _____

2. *Faith in God is spelled R-I-S-K.* Connect with the individual God wants to communicate with and first explain to him or her about the exercise you are doing.

3. *Look for patterns.* Record any patterns you notice, including how you felt prior to asking, during receiving and interpreting the picture, and after sharing it with the person. Make sure to include the way you received God's message and the way you received the interpretation.

4. *Don't fill in the gaps.* Only share with the person exactly what you believe God gave you. Don't share any interpretation of it yet. Give the person time to fill in the gaps. Once the person is finished sharing what the picture means to him or her, then share the interpretation you felt as though the Holy Spirit gave you. If the person is unable to fill in any gaps, or if the picture you received does not mean anything to him or her immediately, then share your interpretation. Note whether or not this experience resonated with your participant, and record his or her response.

*Revisit the *New Neural Pathfinder* tool now to track the spiritual progress you made throughout this lesson.

All too often, we treat God as we would a partner in a cohabiting relationship instead of laying our lives down in covenant with Him. The problem with having a full-access pass to the throne of God is that we often wind up in a casual relationship with Him. Bobby Connor, a prophetic friend of mine, puts it like this: "We are too familiar with the God we hardly know." That's exactly right!

Access God's Thoughts and Ideas

The health of our relationship with the Holy Spirit is largely predicated on our ability to hear and submit to the voice of God. John 15:1–16, a rather long yet profound passage of Scripture, speaks about our relationship with God and the importance of not only hearing the voice of the Spirit, but obeying it. Let's divide this passage into three sections so we can take a closer look at what Jesus is revealing. First, look at verses 1–6:

> I am the true vine, and My Father is the vinedresser. Every branch in Me that does not bear fruit, He takes away; and every branch that bears fruit, He prunes it so that it may bear more fruit. You are already clean because of the word which I have spoken to you. Abide in Me, and I in you. As the branch cannot bear fruit of itself unless it abides in the vine, so neither can you unless you abide in Me. I am the vine, you are the branches; he who abides in Me and I in him, he bears much fruit, for apart from Me you can do nothing. If anyone does not abide in Me, he is thrown away as a branch and dries up; and they gather them, and cast them into the fire and they are burned.

Underline the third sentence (verse 3). Why does Jesus say you are already "clean"?

COGNITIVE CONNECTION

Identify the roles of each of the following from John 15:1–6:

God is the _____ .

Jesus is the _____ .

You are the _____ .

COGNITIVE CONNECTION

Circle each use of the word *abide* in this passage of Scripture. In your own words, what do you believe the overall essence of the word *abide* means in the context in which Jesus was using it? From your perspective, how do you "abide" in God's Word?

_____

_____

_____

_____

_____

The word *clean* here is the same Greek root word as *pruned*. In other words, God uses His "word" to prune us back to our place of fruitful revelation and obedience. He hacks off everything (the deadwood) that is overextended and is undermining our divine responsibility and derailing our destiny.

Now look at verses 7–11:

If you abide in Me, and My words abide in you, ask whatever you wish, and it will be done for you. My Father is glorified by this, that you bear much fruit, and so prove to be My disciples. Just as the Father has loved Me, I have also loved you; abide in My love. If you keep My commandments, you will abide in My love; just as I have kept My Father's commandments and abide in His love. These things I have spoken to you so that My joy may be in you, and that your joy may be made full.

Underline the first sentence in this passage (verse 7). What do you believe Jesus means by "ask whatever you wish, and it will be done for you"?

_____

_____

_____

If we take Jesus at His word—"Whatever you ask in My name, that will I do" (John 14:13)—then we have to have a prunable relationship with Him in which we *listen* to Him and let Him *prune off* the things in our hearts and minds that He deems deadwood dangerous.

Finally, look at verses 12–16:

This is My commandment, that you love one another, just as I have loved you. Greater love has no one than this, that one lay down his life for his friends. You are My friends if you do what I command you. No longer do I call you slaves, for the slave does not know what his master is doing; but I have called you friends, for all things that

I have heard from My Father I have made known to you. You did not choose Me but I chose you, and appointed you that you would go and bear fruit, and that your fruit would remain, so that whatever you ask of the Father in My name He may give to you.

Describe what it looks like in your mind to "love one another" as Christ loves you.

> **COGNITIVE CONNECTION**
>
> Jesus calls you His friend if you obey what commandment?

Jesus says in this passage that we are His friends once we learn to obey His commands. This relational transition from slave to friend opens the door for profound revelation in our lives. A slave only knows how to obey his master, but as God's friends, we have a full-access pass to the voice of the Father and can enter into a new relationship that overflows to everyone around us.

Renew Your Mind

In the passage we just dissected, Jesus states the obvious: If a branch is disconnected from the vine, it cannot do anything like grow leaves or produce grapes. So there is an exhortation for us to stay connected and make an effort to have a vibrant, healthy, ongoing relationship with Jesus.

Name one life area in which you currently believe God is pruning you with His Word.

> **COGNITIVE CONNECTION**
>
> List several practical ways that friendship with God would (or does) impact your day-to-day life.
>
> 1.
>
> 2.
>
> 3.

What word has He spoken to you that He is asking you to "abide" in regarding the area you named?

What fruit do you believe your life will bear if you allow God's Word to prune away the areas that are unfruitful? Be as specific as possible.

_____

_____

_____

Build New Neural Pathways

One of the most common reasons we don't hear God on any kind of regular basis is that we don't turn aside from our daily activities to hear Him. Jeremiah prophesied it like this: "You will seek Me and find Me when you search for Me with all your heart" (Jeremiah 29:13). The heart of the matter is really the matter of the heart. God wants us to value our relationship with Him, not treat Him like a cosmic bellhop or a casual friend.

In Module 1 | Lesson 3 we discussed the power of biblical meditation to help build new neural pathways and renew the spirit of your mind. From this point forward in your journey, set aside five to ten minutes a day to meditate on the truth that you are in a friendship with God. Start by asking the Holy Spirit the following question: What is one key to understanding the real You that most people miss? Record His response, and set aside time to meditate on the revelation that He shares with you daily.

_____

_____

_____

_____

*Revisit the *New Neural Pathfinder* tool now to track the spiritual progress you made throughout this lesson.

Engagement Tool

The Top 4

List the top 4 spiritual insights you gained from this module, whether they came from the thoughts in the lessons, the *Cognitive Connection* exercises, the "Renew Your Mind" reflections or the "Build New Neural Pathways" activations.

1. _____

_____

_____

2. _____

_____

_____

3. _____

_____

_____

_____

4. _____

_____

_____

_____

Plan of Action

Create one action step based on the spiritual insights listed above that would demonstrate spiritual intelligence when you apply it to your daily life. Note that a good action step has a *who*, *what*, *how* and *when*. For example, if I learned from this module that seeking understanding on the matters of God is part of how He designed communication with His people to work, I would create an action step like this: "As God speaks to me with symbolism through dreams, visions and the like (*what*), I (*who*) will seek divine wisdom from the Holy Spirit, from Scripture or through wise counsel (*how*) until I have gained an understanding of what I seek (*when*)."

*Note that the *Spiritual Intelligence Quotient (SQ) Assessment* in my SQ book will give you many other specific action steps you can take to further develop, deepen and implement your SQ, based on your score once you take the test.

Module 3

Activating Spiritual Intelligence

The book of Acts is filled with unusual yet powerful stories of God moving on or through His people. There were those who were intoxicated by the Holy Spirit and spoke in tongues. Some experienced several angel-assisted jailbreaks. Paul blinded a guy named Bar-Jesus. The stories go on and on—deliverances, prophecies, prophets, Philip caught up by the Spirit and translated to another city, dead-raisings, the sick healed, miracles . . . it's all there. Jesus said that signs like these will accompany those who believe (see again Mark 16:17–18).

Consider this: Peter and Paul, among the many other Bible heroes whom we still glean from, did not have the Bible as we know it as a plumb line when they walked out their God-anointed callings. There was no way for them to double-check to see if their encounters and experiences were "biblical." They simply had to trust the Spirit within them. I am very thankful we have the Holy Bible, our great source of truth and encouragement. But let's never forget that we host the same Holy Spirit as our predecessors in the faith, and God expects us to learn to discern and become spiritually intelligent.

Write any three works of the Holy Spirit (miracles, prophecy, gifts, etc.) that you would like to experience as God works through you.

1. _____

2. _____

3. _____

List three proactive action steps you can take in the next ninety days that would contribute positively to maturing in a Spirit-filled life.

1. _____

2. _____

3. _____

When you read of the powerful signs that followed Peter, Paul and so many others, you may feel as if you have lost touch relationally with the Holy Spirit, or as if perhaps you don't know Him at all. But I'm here to remind you that Jesus extended an invitation to you to receive power from on high. Should you accept His invitation, you will find that the Spirit-filled life is the life you were destined for!

*For additional insights into module 3, read chapters 6–9 of my book *Spiritual Intelligence*.

Module 3 | Lesson 1—Discernment of Spirits

The voice of God is the catalyst for everything we do in life. But we have an enemy that is working overtime to distort the voice of God, disrupt the air waves of communication and ultimately destroy us on every level—spirit, soul and body! Is it possible to discern the difference between good and evil? Absolutely. In fact, I know so. Let's dive into spiritual intelligence about how to use discernment for this.

Access God's Thoughts and Ideas

In chapter 6 of *Spiritual Intelligence*, I wrote about how fewer than five decades ago the computer was invented, giving us full access to a genius in a box, with an answer to nearly any question we could ever ask. The potential to solve literally millions of humanity's problems through technology was wild—even stunning! But along with invention and innovation came hackers, pirates and thieves. Shortly after the very first software rolled out of production, a virus was created to destroy it.

The spirit realm is likewise riddled with hackers and pirates who, for various reasons such as selfishness, deception or even downright wickedness, partner with the thief, Satan, to destroy people's lives. The unnerving truth is that spiritual hackers and pirates are highly deceptive, meaning they appear good or maybe even godly at times. Jesus gave so many warnings about people who are operating under the power of a delusional spirit: "For false Christs and false prophets will arise, and will show signs and wonders, in order to lead astray, if possible, the elect" (Mark 13:22).

Fortunately for us, God has given us a supernatural solution with which to expose and disarm the counterfeit. It's called the gift of discernment of spirits (see 1 Corinthians 12:10). The gift of discernment gives us the ability to discern the unseen beings that we are cohabiting this earth with—a vital function in developing our spiritual intelligence. It's a gift available to every

COGNITIVE CONNECTION

Read John 10:10. Whom does Jesus attribute death-dealing behavior to, and how does He describe him?

_____

_____

_____

_____

_____

_____

_____

Who is your hope in the midst of this destructive dynamic that we see in the world, and what does He offer?

_____

_____

_____

_____

_____

_____

_____

_____

believer, and it empowers us to discern between any and all spirits individually.

I believe this gift is one of the most undervalued yet beneficial gifts that serve the Body of Christ. If applied correctly, it would eliminate a great deal of spiritual warfare. It empowers believers to distinguish between what's real and what's false. To clarify, it is not merely discernment, or wisdom, for that matter, nor is it distinguishing only evil spirits. When believers function in this gift in a healthy way, and as God intended, they arise as the solution-driven peacemakers that they are, and they begin the work of recovering, reconciling and restoring those whom the enemy has attempted to kill, steal from and destroy.

People who are influenced by demonic spirits with the intention to deceive are operating in high levels of spiritual intelligence, too. But that kind of SQ is rooted in the thief and is motivated by the wrong spirit. Not only does the gift of discernment give us access to learning which spirit is in operation, but it also exposes the motive and scheme of the spirit.

Take a look at a New Testament example in Acts 16:16–18 of the spirit of divination in operation:

> It happened that as we were going to the place of prayer, a slave-girl having a spirit of divination met us, who was bringing her masters much profit by fortune-telling. Following after Paul and us, she kept crying out, saying, "These men are bond-servants of the Most High God, who are proclaiming to you the way of salvation." She continued doing this for many days. But Paul was greatly annoyed, and turned and said to the spirit, "I command you in the name of Jesus Christ to come out of her!" And it came out at that very moment.

It is important to note here that psychics, sorcerers, palm readers and astrologers often get the information right, but their source is still bent on deception because the thief is lurking with evil intent in the background.

What are your thoughts as to why a demonic spirit would want to reveal who Paul was by shouting it in the streets?

_____

_____

_____

_____

Circle Paul's response to the slave-girl. Why do you feel the disciples were confident (for the most part) when encountering demonic spirits during their assignments?

_____

_____

_____

_____

> ### COGNITIVE CONNECTION
>
> What spirit does Luke (the author of Acts) say the slave-girl is possessed by?
>
> _____
>
> Underline what the slave-girl was shouting as she followed Paul and the disciples around for days. Was she telling the truth or lying?
>
> _____

I want to reiterate here that there are false healers, just as there are false teachers, false prophets, false signs, false wonders and false believers. Much like Moses' encounter with Pharaoh's sorcerers, the false is unleashed on the world to compete with the real, authentic power of God. This is a demonic military strategy meant to confuse people, dilute the truth and resist God's purposes in people's lives.

This is where spiritual intelligence and the art of thinking like God come into play. The gift of discernment was key to Paul and the disciples not only understanding what spirit was influencing the girl, but also gaining insight into what the spirit's motivation was for following them and publicly revealing who they were.

It is vital for us to understand that Jesus commissioned us to root out posers and demonstrate the superior power of the Kingdom of God. We are anointed, equipped and deployed to "destroy the works of the devil" and bring God's authentic goodness everywhere we go. Consider this: If we abandon spiritual intelligence, the nations will be discipled by the thief. To that, I say, "Not on my watch!"

Renew Your Mind

From some believers' perspective—because they don't know how to tell the spiritually real from the fake—the "safe" solution is simply to remove all burden of responsibility by way of abandoning all SQ, miracles and supernatural acts. What believers like this don't realize is that it plays right into the devil's hands. Their fearful reaction to the things of the Spirit creates powerless believers who preach a powerless gospel to a people in bondage to a powerful thief.

Jesus, however, said that supernatural signs will accompany those who believe. Make an honest assessment of where your heart is. Do you trust the Holy Spirit to guide you and lead you into all truth, to the point that you feel confident to lay hands on the sick, pray for the lost, prophesy over the brokenhearted, cast out demons and so on?

It is likely that you know what your biblical response to this question ought to be. But truly take time with the Holy Spirit and have an openhearted conversation. Record the fruit of this conversation here:

_____

_____

_____

_____

_____

If there is any fear encroaching on your spiritual identity, gifts or responsibility as a believer, take a moment, as

---

COGNITIVE CONNECTION

Have you ever had a supernatural experience that left you feeling leery, uncertain or confused? Recall and record it here:

_____

_____

_____

_____

_____

Allow the Holy Spirit to teach you how to discern the spirit behind that experience. Ask if this experience was a manifestation of Him that perhaps was new to you and left you feeling unsure, or if it was motivated by a wrong spirit. Record any impressions, insights or Scriptures the Holy Spirit may bring to mind to help you process this encounter.

Remember, this exercise is aimed at developing your SQ, so be patient, persistent and openhearted to the Holy Spirit's guidance.

_____

_____

_____

_____

Paul did with the slave-girl, to cast out the presence of fear that is attempting to overshadow and steal your authority as a child of God. Stay present with the Holy Spirit, and He will guide you into dismantling any lofty lie that has attached itself to the way you function as a Spirit-filled believer. Record the result of this experience here:

_____

_____

_____

_____

_____

Build New Neural Pathways

It's true that learning to live in the Spirit and be led by the Spirit can be messy. Spiritual intelligence comes at a cost. You and I will make many mistakes as we learn and grow in the Lord—that's for sure. Yet personally, I would rather take the risk of living out God's power instead of reducing my experience in the Spirit down to something I can control.

The only way forward in spiritual intelligence is deeper in! Would you like to develop the gift of discernment in your life in a healthy way? Would you like to disarm fear and walk hand in hand with the Spirit of peace? If so, first ask the Holy Spirit to give you the gift of discernment. Second, start developing this gift by discerning the spirits that are influencing your thought life. For example, you could start with your attitude over something like finances. If you are married, notice what happens when you and your spouse begin to talk about money. Does your conversation get heated fast, or do you notice that it is solution driven?

COGNITIVE CONNECTION

Describe how the gift of discernment could potentially help you in your day-to-day life.

_____

_____

_____

_____

_____

_____

Now let's go to the source—the Holy Spirit. Take a moment and ask Him what Spirit-filled insight He would like to share with you about the gift of discernment. Record your time with the Holy Spirit here:

_____

_____

_____

_____

_____

Begin to discern the spirit behind what may be influencing your own emotions and thought life in an area first. If you stick with it, I believe you will begin to notice an incredible improvement in your overall sense of well-being in all areas as you begin to discern the Spirit of peace, who will be present.

Choose one life area in which you would like to use the gift of discernment. It could be your relationships, health and wellness, career, finances, your calling or some other area. Over the next seven days, note any significant detail in your thought life or emotional health that is triggered around the area you chose. Ask the Holy Spirit to help you discern the spirit behind your reaction. Use the lines below as a log to record the area and the thoughts or emotions you discover in yourself that are centering around it.

Life area: _____

Day 1 _____

_____

_____

Day 2 _____

_____

_____

Day 3 _____

_____

_____

Day 4 _____

_____

_____

Day 5 _____

_____

_____

Day 6 _____

_____

_____

Day 7 _____

_____

_____

*Revisit the *New Neural Pathfinder* tool now to track the spiritual progress you made throughout this lesson. Don't forget to write "using the gift of discernment" in one of the blank lines on the pathfinder tool so you can continue to track your consecutive progress on it.

| **Lesson 2—The Three Heavens**

In the last lesson, we learned how to push past spiritual deceivers by using the gift of discernment so that we can operate with spiritual intelligence. I propose that to have ultimate success, however, we must understand our spiritual seat, or the position from which we rule and think.

Access God's Thoughts and Ideas

Did you know that the Bible talks about three different heavens? The three heavens represent levels of power—the first heaven having the power of mere humanity, the second heaven having the power of the disruptive devil and his defunct cavalry of demons, and the third heaven carrying the authority and power of God Himself. Let's take a biblical look at these three heavens.

1. *First heaven:* "In the beginning God created the *heavens and the earth*" (Genesis 1:1, emphasis added). This *first heaven* is the visible world, the dimension that our five senses are acutely tuned in to, the natural realm that we are all aware of and interact with on a daily basis.

2. *Second heaven:* "Our struggle is not against flesh and blood, but against the rulers, against the powers, against the world forces of this darkness, against the spiritual forces of wickedness in the *heavenly places*" (Ephesians 6:12, emphasis added). Notice the apostle Paul said that there are evil forces in *heavenly places*. Let's be clear: There are no demonic, satanic or evil forces in God's heaven. Thus, we call this realm from which Satan rules the *second heaven*.

3. *Third heaven:* "I know a man in Christ who fourteen years ago—whether in the body I do not know, or out of the body I do not know, God knows—such a man was caught up to the *third heaven*. And I know how such a

COGNITIVE CONNECTION

Read Ephesians 2:1–7. According to verse 6, God has seated us with Christ Jesus where?

_____

Considering what we just learned about the three heavens, is verse 6 referring to the first, second or third heaven?

_____

In your own words, write out what it means that Christ has seated you in the third heaven with Him. How might this third-heaven reality impact your first-heaven experience?

_____

_____

_____

_____

_____

_____

_____

_____

man—whether in the body or apart from the body I do not know, God knows—was caught up into Paradise and heard inexpressible words, which a man is not permitted to speak" (2 Corinthians 12:2–4, emphasis added). Paul reveals through his own spiritual experience that there is a _third heaven_ two levels above our earthly experience and one level above the satanic realm.

So many Christians live reactively from earth (the first heaven) toward heaven (the third heaven), instead of living from heaven toward earth. In chapter 7 of _Spiritual Intelligence_, I discuss in depth the fruit of believers not taking their seat in the third heaven with Christ. If we abandon our third-heaven seat, we sublet our authority to a de-authorized devil and consequently commission the second heaven to rule the world. Then the human race becomes subject to the second heaven. I want to remind you that as believers we are not victims; nor are we a subservient subculture suffering under the power of worldly people who have relegated their life to pretentious and perverted deceptions.

1. Think about your current life circumstances and write down a first-heaven problem that needs a third-heaven solution. It might be a physical health problem, a relational issue or a daily life problem like finances. (For example, "There is not enough money coming in to meet the needs of my family.") First-heaven problem:

_____

_____

_____

2. What first-heaven solution(s) have you applied to the first-heaven problem you listed above? What were the results? (For example, "I've taken a second job and my bills are covered, but my stress level has increased. Now I'm fighting with my spouse, and my family is suffering.")

_____

_____

_____

_____

_____

COGNITIVE CONNECTION

It is imperative that, as believers, we understand that we cannot solve first-heaven problems with humanity's first-heaven solutions. Why? Because the demonic forces of the second heaven are actually creating the root issues. We must have God's third-heaven resolutions to our world's first-heaven issues, or we relegate our world to second-heaven domination.

3. In the previous lesson, we learned that God has given us the gift of discernment. Using this gift, expose any spirit, demonic mindsets or root lies that originate from the second heaven and may be compounding your current challenge. Take a moment to discern whether or not the demonic realm is working against your personal life. Write out what the Holy Spirit shows you about any second-heaven influence here. (For example, "I uncovered that I believe a root lie: _Poverty is my portion_. This mindset has perpetuated a cycle of poverty throughout my family for multiple generations. Though struggling is all I have known, this is not God's portion for me. This lie has prevented me from seeing my value and has robbed me of God-given opportunities.")

_____

_____

_____

_____

_____

4. The Lord has invited us to live from our heavenly throne toward our earthly dwelling so that we can profoundly shift the course of history toward His prosperous Kingdom. There are hundreds of biblical examples of third-heaven solutions being used to solve first-heaven problems. We find one such example in Matthew 17, when Jesus told Peter to pay taxes for the two of them this way: "Go to the sea and throw in a hook, and take the first fish that comes up; and when you open its mouth, you will find a shekel. Take that and give it to them for you and Me" (verse 27). How profound this is! Accessing the mind of God, Jesus saw in real time where He could find money to cover the taxes. This is spiritual intelligence in action. Using the first-heaven problem you listed above, now exercise your God-given spiritual intelligence. (Remember, you are seated in the third heaven with Christ. He has done the hard work.) Ask the Holy Spirit to reveal to you a third-heaven solution for your first-heaven problem. Write whatever you hear, see or discern. Third-heaven solution:

_____

_____

_____

_____

_____

_____

_____

_____

5. Based on what the Holy Spirit revealed to you above, what action step of faith do you need to take? (For example, Peter went fishing to catch the fish that held the tax payment in its mouth.)

_____

_____

_____

_____

Speaking of third-heaven revelation and divine wisdom, the apostle Paul wrote this:

> To me, the very least of all saints, this grace was given, to preach to the Gentiles the unfathomable riches of Christ, and to bring to light what is the administration of the mystery which for ages has been hidden in God who created all things; so that the manifold wisdom of God might now be made known through the church to the rulers and the authorities in the heavenly places.
>
> Ephesians 3:8–10

We have been commissioned, called and equipped to display the "manifold wisdom of God" to *rulers* and *authorities* in heavenly places. Note that Paul is not talking about teaching demonic princes in the second heaven; he is referring to angelic principalities who abide in the third heaven and are assigned to co-labor with us in our divine mission. These angels on assignment are waiting to serve you as you carry out God's plans and purposes!

Is it starting to set in that you are God's "solutionary," commissioned to take third-heaven revelations and solve earth's first-heaven challenges? I hope you are beginning to understand just how significantly blessed, glorious and powerful Jesus has created you to be as someone who can help bring third-heaven answers to the world's first-heaven problems.

Renew Your Mind

As I talked about in chapter 7 of the book, where you "sit" matters. If you are one of those practical people, I can hear you groaning, *How do I know if I'm living from earth or from heaven?* You can look for certain symptoms in your life that will reveal where you are "seated" spiritually. Below are seven symptoms that reveal you are living from *earth* toward *heaven*. Check any and all that apply to you.

_____ 1. You worry a lot.

_____ 2. You feel like a powerless victim, and you have a big devil and a little God.

_____ 3. You don't think you have anything to contribute to making the world a better place.

_____ 4. You're convinced that every year the world is getting worse.

_____ 5. All your prayers are in reaction to a bad circumstance.

_____ 6. You have no vision for the future.

_____ 7. You struggle with low self-esteem and a poverty mentality.

Below are seven symptoms that reveal you are living from *heaven* toward *earth*. Check any and all that apply to you.

_____ 1. You believe God can do the impossible, and you think like He does.

_____ 2. You live with a one-hundred-year vision and plan to leave a legacy to your children's children.

_____ 3. The world's troubles only serve to challenge you to think big and bring God's ideas to the table.

_____ 4. You view devil encounters as a compliment to the fact that you are doing something worth resisting, and you see these encounters as opportunities to win.

_____ 5. You know you are a son or daughter of the King; therefore, you carry yourself like royalty.

_____ 6. The commission to disciple nations positively affects your prayer life as you shape history on your knees.

_____ 7. You look for God's perspective on current events, and you refuse to let the media or a political or religious spirit shape your mindset or cloud your worldview.

Based on your answers, are you living more from earth toward heaven, or from heaven toward earth?

Build New Neural Pathways

It is time to step up into your heavenly seat, if that is not where you are living from already. Jesus is waiting for you. He has made a place for you on the throne. He is excited for you to experience using the authority He purchased for you on the cross!

Shift your perspective on your "seat" by listing seven personal declarations you will make as someone who is seated in heaven with Christ, looking down at your life's challenges. (For example, "I will experience God's favor in my life, along with divinely ordained opportunities and connections. This will break the cycle of poverty off my life and legacy, which will affect future generations to come.")

1. _____

_____

_____

2. _____

_____

_____

3. _____

_____

_____

4. _____

5. _____

6. _____

7. _____

Copy your third-heaven declarations onto sticky notes or pieces of paper and tape them up individually in places where you will see them regularly (on your bathroom mirror, in your car, at your desk, etc.). Doing this will refocus and reframe your reality throughout the day as you read and declare them again and again.

Remember, you will disempower the enemy! You will overcome first-heaven challenges with third-heaven solutions! You are God's solutionary!

* Revisit the *New Neural Pathfinder* tool now to track the spiritual progress you made throughout this lesson.

Christ came as the Light of the world, and He wants us to take His light—Christ in you and me, the hope of glory—and reflect it to the rest of the world (see John 8:12; Colossians 1:27). The prophet Isaiah put it this way:

> Arise, shine; for your light has come, and the glory of the LORD has risen upon you. For behold, darkness will cover the earth and deep darkness the peoples; but the LORD will rise upon you and His glory will appear upon you. Nations will come to your light, and kings to the brightness of your rising.
>
> Isaiah 60:1–3

Access God's Thoughts and Ideas

I want to take you on a third-heaven, revelatory journey through some of the most powerful Scriptures ever inspired by the Holy Spirit. Please read the following passage slowly and consider its life-changing—maybe even world-changing—impact. The apostle Paul writes,

> I pray that the eyes of your heart may be enlightened, so that you will know what is the hope of His calling, what are the riches of the glory of His inheritance in the saints, and what is the surpassing greatness of His power toward us who believe. These are in accordance with the working of the strength of His might which He brought about in Christ, when He raised Him from the dead and seated Him at His right hand in the heavenly places, far above all rule and authority and power and dominion, and every name that is named, not only in this age but also in the one to come. And He put all things in subjection under His feet, and gave Him as head over all things to the church, which is His body, the fullness of Him who fills all in all.
>
> Ephesians 1:18–23

COGNITIVE CONNECTION

In verse 18, Paul prays that the eyes of your heart may be _____ . The English word *enlighten* in this passage is translated from the Greek word *photizo*. We get our English word *photosynthesis* from this Greek word, which describes the process plants use to convert light energy to chemical energy to fuel those organisms' activity. Paul is praying that God's light would *photizo* in our hearts, or maybe more clearly, that His light would fuel us . . . converting light to revelation. This transformation by revelation is what empowers us to radiate the Kingdom of God in all aspects of our lives.

Following Paul's prayer that our hearts would be enlightened, what are the three specific insights from the first sentence that Paul prays for us to receive revelation in?

1. _____

2. _____

3. _____

Paul said that these three insights he prayed for us to receive (our calling, inheritance and power) are "in accordance with" (verse 19) the following four truths:

1. "The working of the strength of His might, which He brought about in Christ, when He raised Him from the dead" (verses 19–20). When God raised Jesus from the dead, we believers *all* rose with Him.

2. The Father "seated Him at His right hand in the heavenly places, far above all rule and authority and power and dominion, and every name that is named, not only in this age but also in the one to come" (verses 20–21). Our heavenly Father positioned Jesus *far above all* rule and authority and power and dominion.

3. "He put all things in subjection under His feet" (verse 22). In other words, the most insignificant believer in the Body of Christ still has authority over the most powerful evil principality in the cosmos!

4. "He gave Him as head over all things to the church, which is His body, the fullness of Him who fills all in all" (verses 22–23). Our identity in God stands on the shoulders of the truth that everything is under Jesus' feet and He is in charge.

These four truths are to the spirit world what the laws of physics are to the natural world. It is simply impossible to understand the power of the Gospel and the authority of the believer in Christ without truly grasping the full revelation of this declaration.

In your own words, how do these spiritual truths impact spiritual intelligence and empower us to live a life free of fear?

_____

_____

_____

_____

The passage of Scripture we just unpacked lays the foundation of spiritual intelligence: It is not just that we can *see*, but that we *become* "the light of the world" on humanity—the very essence of God's revelation (see Matthew 5:14). When our hearts are enlightened by way of the Holy Spirit, God's light transforms us, but His divine purpose is that His light also works *through* us.

Renew Your Mind

Understand that God is not just revealing truth to us; He is putting the "Spirit of revelation" in us so that we become the revealers of truth. He is giving us spiritual intelligence in a way that will attract the world!

In your own words, how do you believe the revelation of the Gospel has transformed your personal relationship with Jesus?

_____

_____

_____

_____

How has your relationship with Jesus transformed the way you see yourself?

_____

_____

_____

_____

_____

_____

_____

In what ways have you noticed that the relationship you have with Jesus, and with yourself because of Him, attracts others to you because of His light?

_____

_____

_____

_____

_____

_____

_____

Build New Neural Pathways

You are a spiritually intelligent person who has been given the "Spirit of revelation" so that you can, as Matthew 5:14 puts it, be "the light of the world." You will shift the course of your life and your legacy profoundly, and you will change the course of history as you arise and you shine forth the light God has given you.

One of the most spiritually intelligent things we can do is love God and love people—not passively, but passionately, pursuing our connections with courage and humility. Take a moment and think of one friend, neighbor, family member or co-worker who has always been on your "acquaintance" list, but with whom you have never pursued a friendship. The Holy Spirit will bring someone to mind. Have you ever considered that the person is drawn to the Light of the God that dwells within you? Write the person's name here:

_____

Take time to pray for that person. Ask the Holy Spirit to share one thing He loves about him or her and one attribute that very few other people recognize. Write that thing or attribute here:

_____

_____

_____

Consider sharing this prophetic insight with that person. If you feel called to share, do not add anything to what God gave you or take anything away from it. If you do not share your insight with that person, over the course of several days at least begin to declare over the person through prayer how God sees him or her. Allow your enlightened heart to prophesy and declare God's love over the person you named.

*Revisit the *New Neural Pathfinder* tool now to track the spiritual progress you made throughout this lesson.

The life-changing side of spiritual intelligence is always catalyzed through relationships between God and His people. In a relational transfer of information, a dynamic takes place in which the recipient experiences transformation in his or her inner person. Literally, information comes alive in the context of specific kinds of relationships. Let me illustrate this with these words of Jesus: "A pupil is not above his teacher; but everyone, after he has been fully trained, will be like his teacher" (Luke 6:40).

Access God's Thoughts and Ideas

When information is delivered through the context of discipleship, we are not just learning; we are becoming like the One who teaches us—in this case, like Jesus.

The Parable of the Sower emphasizes this. Jesus taught us that the Kingdom is planted in the lives of people, just as a sower plants seeds in his field. The three main elements in this parable are the sower, who is God, the seed, which is the Kingdom, and the soil, which represents our hearts. Look at Matthew 13:20–21:

> The one on whom seed was sown on the rocky places, this is the man who hears the word and immediately receives it with joy; yet he has no firm root in himself, but is only temporary, and when affliction or persecution arises because of the word, immediately he falls away.

The Greek word here for *seed* is the word *sperma*, which means "offspring." We get our English word *sperm* from this word. Notice how the seed that falls on rocky soil is described as falling on a man who has "no firm root in himself." He was not prepared to nurture and develop the seed. It may seem odd that someone has to prepare to receive the Kingdom, until you realize that the Kingdom is being transferred in the form of a seed or sperm. Let's examine this a little further to gain some understanding of the process.

In Galatians 4:19, Paul says something interesting: "My children, with whom I am again in labor until Christ is formed in you." In your own words, what does Paul mean when he says that he labors until Christ is formed in you?

Take a moment to visualize what Christ fully formed in you looks like. Describe what you see:

As I discussed in chapter 9 of *Spiritual Intelligence*, Paul labored among the people through instruction or teaching and preaching, and through correcting believers when they got offtrack. He was helping them prepare their hearts for the Kingdom of God. The word *instruction* actually means "structures formed in me." In other words, instruction fashions a sort of womb within us so that we can receive "teaching," which in the context of this kind of spiritual intelligence is "information," or more accurately, "the Kingdom forming within us." Paul was a sower, sowing the seed of the Kingdom into the "wombs" of his people until the word was fully formed within them!

Let me share with you a couple of Hebrew words that will help you understand how to prepare your heart to receive the Word of God and develop your SQ further.

1. The Hebrew word *musar* and the Greek word *paideia* are most often translated "instruction" in our English Bible. They mean "discipline, chastening, correction, punishment, reproof and warning." The implication is that instruction is education or training through disciplinary action. That's why we are called *disciples*. The word *disciple* means "learner," but it comes from the word *discipline*.

2. The Hebrew word *leqach* and the Greek word *didasko* are most often translated "to teach" or "teaching" in our English Bible. They mean "to persuade, learn or receive." Teaching is literally the process of receiving revelation, and it is the gathering of information.

Now let's go back to the story of the sower in Matthew 13. Jesus said that the man representing the rocky places had no roots in himself, so the seed died. Roots are formed through the ability to receive instruction, or "structures within." If we refuse instruction, correction, reproof or discipline, we won't form a "womb" in which to nurture and develop the seed of God's Word within us.

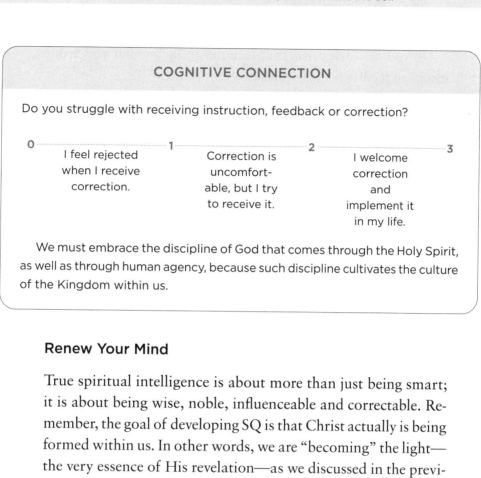

COGNITIVE CONNECTION

Do you struggle with receiving instruction, feedback or correction?

0	1	2	3
I feel rejected when I receive correction.	Correction is uncomfort-able, but I try to receive it.	I welcome correction and implement it in my life.	

We must embrace the discipline of God that comes through the Holy Spirit, as well as through human agency, because such discipline cultivates the culture of the Kingdom within us.

Renew Your Mind

True spiritual intelligence is about more than just being smart; it is about being wise, noble, influenceable and correctable. Remember, the goal of developing SQ is that Christ actually is being formed within us. In other words, we are "becoming" the light—the very essence of His revelation—as we discussed in the previous lesson.

Can you recall the first memory you have of experiencing correction of any type? Was it a positive or negative experience?

_____

_____

What belief have you formed about yourself based on this experience?

_____

_____

_____

_____

Do you have life areas that lack discipline or that you avoid receiving feedback in? Explain:

_____

_____

_____

_____

_____

Build New Neural Pathways

The questions you just completed in the "Renew Your Mind" section have positioned you like a farmer who is assessing the condition of the soil—your heart. Now prepare the soil of your heart to receive God's divine guidance when it comes to your beliefs about correction, whether it comes through Him or in your daily relationships with others. Do this by using the gift of discernment that you asked God for in lesson 1 of this module.

With the help of the Holy Spirit, and using the gift of discernment, is there any spirit that has attached itself to your openness to receive correction or constructive feedback? Write whatever you discern, hear or see:

_____

_____

_____

_____

Based on what you just received from God, what action do you need to take today that will open up your heart and allow the Holy Spirit or those you are in relationships with to sow seeds of the Kingdom in you by way of instruction, correction or discipline?

Implement this action in your life this week and take note of the new "structures within" that are being formed in your heart. Intentionally welcome feedback and constructive criticism, and look for practical ways to implement discipline in your life.

*Revisit the *New Neural Pathfinder* tool now to track the spiritual progress you made throughout this lesson.

Engagement Tool

The Top 4

List the top 4 spiritual insights you gained from this module, whether they came from the thoughts in the lessons, the *Cognitive Connection* exercises, the "Renew Your Mind" reflections or the "Build New Neural Pathways" activations.

1. _____

   _____

   _____

   _____

2. _____

   _____

   _____

   _____

3. _____

   _____

   _____

   _____

4. _____

   _____

   _____

   _____

Plan of Action

Create one action step based on the spiritual insights listed above that would demonstrate spiritual intelligence when you apply it to your daily life. Note that a good action step has a *who, what, how* and *when*. For example, if one takeaway from this module is that by engaging my SQ, I can solve first-heaven problems with third-heaven solutions, an action step I might create would be: "As a challenge presents itself in real time (*what* and *when*), I (*who*) will discern and dispel any demonic influence and will pursue divine wisdom proactively (*how*) until a resolution has come, since I am one of God's solutionaries (*who*)."

*Note that the *Spiritual Intelligence Quotient (SQ) Assessment* in my SQ book will give you many other specific action steps you can take to further develop, deepen and implement your SQ, based on your score once you take the test.

Module 4

The Physics of SQ

People who have little or no experience with SQ often pen so much of what is written about life in the Spirit. Many ministers travel the world and speak about ethereal philosophies that, frankly, they have never walked out in their own lives. At the end of the day, however, our faith must actually *work*. The apostle John wrote, "The Word became flesh, and dwelt among us" (John 1:14). In my mind, the ultimate test of truth is, Can you dress it up in flesh? Does it equal an experience, or is it just words, intellectual ideas or vain philosophies?

The apostle Paul became tired of the Church being stuck in an eternal loop of theories, lofty ideas and ethereal speculations. He wrote the following warning to the first-century believers in the Greek city of Corinth: "I will come to you soon, if the Lord wills, and I shall find out, not the words of those who are arrogant but their power. For the kingdom of God does not consist in words but in power" (1 Corinthians 4:19–20).

Name one time that God asked you to step out in faith and the result defied all logic or reason. Explain:

———————————————————————————

———————————————————————————

———————————————————————————

———————————————————————————

When was the last time you shared a personal testimony with someone about encountering God's power? Or do you consider sharing your faith to be more centered around the theological points of your perspective?

———————————————————————————

———————————————————————————

———————————————————————————

———————————————————————————

———————————————————————————

———————————————————————————

In this part of the study, I'd like to teach you how to tap into spiritual intelligence that actually has practical applications for everyday life, because it is true that a person with an argument has no power over a person with an experience.

*For additional insights into module 4, read chapters 10–13 of my book *Spiritual Intelligence*.

Lesson 1—The Law of Faith

Do you remember when Jesus put His disciples in a boat and sent them to the other side of the Sea of Galilee? Then they saw Him trotting out on the water in the midst of a bad storm and thought He was a ghost. When they freaked out, Jesus told them, "Take courage; it is I, do not be afraid" (Matthew 14:27). Then Peter suddenly had this brilliant idea and yelled, "Lord, if it is You, command me to come to You on the water" (verse 28). What Peter likely did not understand at the time was that he was about to exercise faith that transcended the laws of physics!

Access God's Thoughts and Ideas

Have you ever noticed how Peter never seemed to be the sharpest knife in the drawer? Regardless of the size of his IQ, however, the guy had guts—or even better, he had SQ. Peter possessed a special kind of spiritual intelligence rooted in faith and inspired by courage. What I glean from Peter walking on water with Jesus is that Peter refused to be satisfied with spiritual principles that had no practical application. You know what happened next. Peter got out of the boat! After all, what good is spiritual intelligence if it has no purpose?

It is important that we don't miss the main message of Peter walking on water with Jesus: Faith caused Peter to tap into the third-heaven, superior law of the Spirit. However brief the moment, he experienced the Kingdom come near him. Walking on water, he demonstrated that faith is the on-ramp to experiencing a superior ecosystem manifesting over an inferior ecosystem.

In fact, everything in the spirit realm works by the *law of faith*, whether someone is operating from the dark side (out of the second heaven) or from God's Spirit (out of the third heaven). Faith is the foundational element of everything in the spirit world.

Let's dive a little deeper into the *law of faith*. Do you recall the story in Matthew 17:16–20 when Jesus comes down from the Mount of Transfiguration only to be greeted by a desperate

COGNITIVE CONNECTION

Read Jesus' response again out loud, this time substituting the word *briefness* for *littleness*: "Because of the _____ of your faith; for truly I say to you, if you have faith the size of a mustard seed, you will say to this mountain, 'Move from here to there,' and it will move; and nothing will be impossible to you."

father begging Him to heal his severely demonized son, whom Jesus' disciples could not heal? Remember Jesus' response to the disciples about why they could not drive out the demon and heal the boy? He told them, "Because of the littleness of your faith; for truly I say to you, if you have faith the size of a mustard seed, you will say to this mountain, 'Move from here to there,' and it will move; and nothing will be impossible to you" (verse 20). The word *littleness* in this passage is the Greek word *oligos*, meaning "brief," and also "little way, little while, short time."

When we read Jesus' response to the disciples with the right understanding, it shows us that Jesus is not referring to the *amount* of faith they had (or we have). Instead, He is referring to *how long* they (or we) hang on to faith in the midst of the fight. How does this change your perspective about operating in the law of faith?

_____

_____

_____

Ultimately, we cannot grow our faith on the deck of a ship. We can spend our life watching other "water walkers," hearing their stories and reading their books, but the only way we will grow our own water-walking faith is to step out of our sophisticated philosophies and practice transferring things from the third heaven to the visible world by faith.

In other words, if you really want to move that mountain that stands between you and your destiny as a supernatural, spiritually intelligent child of God, then you are going to have to believe persistently in the impossible.

Renew Your Mind

Solomon wrote, "Hope deferred makes the heart sick, but desire fulfilled is a tree of life" (Proverbs 13:12). It is not deferring what we hoped for that makes our hearts sick; it is deferring our *hope* itself that makes us sick. When we stop hoping, we get sick.

The gravity of all the laws of the Spirit rests on faith, yet as I said, faith rests on experiencing hope for something. Hope feels; it doesn't see. It is the earnest expectation that something good is about to happen. Hope does not know what's going to happen; it just knows something will. Once hope creates expectation, faith begins to "look" for the thing hope is feeling.

Is there something in your life that you have been hoping and believing for faithfully, but you have not seen the fruit of your faith for it yet?

_____

_____

Do you detect any sense of your hope being deferred? How is this different from the thing itself being deferred, while hope remains?

_____

_____

_____

Regarding what you are believing for, are you open to inviting others to join you in faith for whatever you wrote? Communicate this with the people you named in Module 2 | Lesson 2. Ask them to join you faithfully in prayer for as long as it takes.

· ·

*If your answer is yes to feeling that your hope has been deferred, I also encourage you to read the story of Olive in chapter 11 of *Spiritual Intelligence* (if you haven't already), and then reread the sections titled "Hope Deferred" and "The Fight for Hope," where I discuss this further.

COGNITIVE CONNECTION

Hebrews 11:1–3 tells us, "Now faith is the assurance of things hoped for, the conviction of things not seen. For by it the men of old gained approval. By faith we understand that the worlds were prepared by the word of God, so that what is seen was not made out of things which are visible." How does the Hebrews writer describe faith in the first verse?

_____

_____

In other words, the seedbed of faith is hope. The way I see it, hope feels, faith sees and love never fails! You cannot have faith without first experiencing hope for something that is not yet tangible, which then activates your faith to be able to visualize it, and opens your mouth to declare it.

This passage of Hebrews says it is by faith that we understand that the worlds were not made out of things visible, but were prepared by what?

_____

The invisible became visible by the force of faith. As I say in chapter 11 of the book, faith is the foundation of spiritual intelligence and the holy grail of the mystery of creation. Faith actualizes dreams, on-ramps visions and overcomes visible obstacles.

COGNITIVE CONNECTION

If you've made it this far into the workbook, you've already experienced some moments when I asked you to step out in faith as a result of what you were learning. Those steps require courage. Yet when confronted with faith-defining moments, are you more apt to "step out of the boat," or do you have a tendency to formulate spiritual excuses to sidestep the moment? If it is ever the latter, write out an example of a spiritual excuse that you might use to prevent yourself from operating in faith.

_____

_____

_____

_____

What do you believe the root fear is behind your excuse?

_____

_____

_____

_____

What does Jesus say about your root fear?

_____

_____

_____

_____

_____

Build New Neural Pathways

In chapter 3 of _Spiritual Intelligence_ and in Module 1 | Lesson 4 here, I shared one of my favorite miracle stories about Elisha and the widow's oil. This story points out that most of the supernatural provisions in the Bible occurred in response to people's pure desperation, not out of their divine lifestyle. Think about it like this: If Elisha had had the money to hand over to the widow in need (the EQ answer), he would not have had the experience of turning to God for a real-time supernatural solution (the SQ answer).

When we look at the miraculous ways God supernaturally provided for people in the Bible, we clearly see that physical obedience brought spiritual release. This is no different for us as modern-day believers. When we seek God for a third-heaven answer (SQ) before relegating our thinking to lower-level problem solving (IQ and EQ), we not only are able to bring heaven to earth, but we also quite literally build new neural pathways in our brain that make space for impossibilities becoming realities.

Put your faith to the test. Imagine three ways God could fulfill your hopes—ways that do not fit into the laws of physics, logic and reason!

1. _____

2. _____

3. _____

Consider what kind of physical obedience needs to take place in your life to bring spiritual release. For example, Elisha told the widow to gather all her jars. She responded in obedience, and God moved by filling every jar she had gathered with oil, which she then sold to pay her debt. Seek wisdom from the Holy Spirit about a similar obedient response you can carry out in your situation.

*Revisit the _New Neural Pathfinder_ tool now to track the spiritual progress you made throughout this lesson.

Lesson 2—Spiritual Physics

Have you heard the idiom "If only these walls could talk," which is usually applied to the secret conversations of very important and/or influential people? In the truest sense, God's walls do talk! In fact, everything God made has a voice that begs to whisper the secret mysteries of the Master.

Access God's Thoughts and Ideas

Have you ever considered what takes place when a person experiences a miracle, healing or deliverance? Throughout the gospels the Bible called miracles "signs," the reason being the *way* miracles actually take place.

In your own words, what do you believe is taking place physically when miracles happen? Or as Jesus put it, when "the Kingdom of heaven is at hand."

_____

_____

_____

_____

By way of announcing that the Kingdom of heaven is at hand, Jesus describes in Matthew 10:5–8 the dynamic of a superior ecosystem that has superimposed itself over an inferior ecosystem, resulting in an altered physical condition. So what we call a *miracle* is actually a manifestation of the superior laws of third-heaven physics (called the law of the Spirit), superimposed over the inferior laws of first-heaven physics.

Romans 1:20 says, "For since the creation of the world His invisible attributes, His eternal power and divine nature, have been clearly seen, being understood through what has been made, so that they are without excuse." In other words, the attributes,

COGNITIVE CONNECTION

In Matthew 10:5–8, Jesus sent out the twelve disciples after giving them these instructions:

> Do not go in the way of the Gentiles, and do not enter any city of the Samaritans; but rather go to the lost sheep of the house of Israel. And as you go, preach, saying, "The kingdom of heaven is at hand." Heal the sick, raise the dead, cleanse the lepers, cast out demons. Freely you received, freely give.

What did Jesus tell the disciples to say "is at hand" whenever they performed miracles?

_____

_____

power and nature of the Creator are revealed through His creation.

When a miracle takes place, creation is simply responding to the nature of its Creator and revealing His glory! It is as if first-heaven science becomes God's personal assistant. This leads me to believe that first-heaven science was never meant to be anti-God, but rather pro-revelation.

It is intriguing to think that faith may be the key to first-heaven scientific discoveries and that SQ may unlock the door to the mysteries of creation. Even better than all of that, God has seated us with Christ Jesus to lead the path to these discoveries. The big question is, Do we as believers have the faith and the SQ to step into our role as pioneers in the scientific realm and as God's solutionaries in every area?

To gain even more insight into the spiritual physics behind miracles, we first need to consider a couple of the foundational laws of first-heaven physics—the law of gravity and the law of lift.

- Law of gravity: The simple definition of this law is that "what goes up must come down." In simple terms, if I jump off a roof, there is no negotiating the manifestation of gravity. It's a law. If I jump off a roof, one hundred percent of the time I will hit the ground quickly.

- Law of lift: Put simply, this definition states, "The law of lift overcomes the law of gravity and causes a plane (or many other objects) to rise instead of fall." Like the law of gravity, this one is a law. It's a dynamic rooted in physics that God set in motion when He created the world.

The law of gravity dictates that everything falls toward the earth, but the law of lift is greater than the law of gravity in that it overcomes the law of gravity by causing objects to rise through employing a superior force.

*I discuss these laws and concepts further in chapter 11 of my book *Spiritual Intelligence.*

Now apply this kind of thinking to SQ. Think about a miracle, which, as we learned, is a sign because a superior law of the Spirit has been superimposed over an inferior law of physics in the same way, metaphorically speaking, that the law of lift overcomes the law of gravity. It is important to understand that a miracle is the manifestation of the third heaven's *superior* law of the Spirit.

Now look at Romans 8:1–4:

Therefore there is now no condemnation for those who are in Christ Jesus. For the law of the Spirit of life in Christ Jesus has set you free from the law of sin and of death. For what the Law could not do, weak as it was through the flesh, God did: sending His own Son in the likeness of sinful flesh and as an offering for sin, He condemned sin in the flesh, so that the requirement of the Law might be fulfilled in us, who do not walk according to the flesh but according to the Spirit.

Identify and list the two laws found in this passage of Scripture.

1. _____

2. _____

According to this passage, how have believers been set free from condemnation and the law of sin and death?

_____

_____

_____

_____

Spiritual laws may be superior to the laws of physics, but these laws are no less systematized, organized and structured than the laws of physics. Furthermore, if you

---

COGNITIVE CONNECTION

Considering what we learned about faith in lesson 1 of this module, how do you believe faith is key to scientific discovery?

_____

_____

_____

_____

How do you imagine that the application of spiritual intelligence pioneers new insights into the mysteries of creation?

_____

_____

_____

_____

_____

_____

_____

_____

COGNITIVE CONNECTION

Let's examine for a moment how the spirit realm operates within spiritual laws, just as the physical realm operates within scientific laws. Consider Luke 6:38: "Give, and it will be given to you. They will pour into your lap a good measure—pressed down, shaken together, and running over. For by your standard of measure it will be measured to you in return." Identify two spiritual laws Jesus mentions in this verse and record them here:

1._____

2._____

This verse, which is primarily about generosity, reveals that God has set up a system of spiritual laws that govern generosity: (1) If you give, it will be given to you, and (2) by your measure, it will be measured to you. If you give, God has predetermined by His Word (the same way He spoke the heavens and earth into existence) that it will return in equal measure to you, but multiplied several times over.

are not spiritually intelligent and you don't understand the laws of the Spirit, then you can become a victim of the invisible realm (that second heaven where the enemy is at work). The laws of the Spirit are so written on the hearts of our inner man that even non-Christians recognize them. Yet understanding the *laws* of the Spirit is paramount to being successful in the *life* of the Spirit, which is why developing SQ is important.

Renew Your Mind

In this lesson we examined a couple of spiritual laws regarding generosity, and in chapter 11 of *Spiritual Intelligence* I mention a few more. Name at least three other spiritual laws you can think of that are found throughout Scripture.

1. _____

2. _____

3. _____

I encourage you to begin highlighting laws of the Spirit as you read your Bible. This exercise will bring you profound insight into developing your SQ and renewing your mind about how life in the Spirit works.

Build New Neural Pathways

The science of the Spirit is not complex, yet what makes it mysterious is that many of us have ignored this third-heaven realm most of our lives. To apply the laws of the Spirit as you develop your SQ, you will need an enlightened heart and an appetite for developing your life in the Spirit. But I have good news for you: Jesus has given you the Holy Spirit, so everything you need in developing your understanding of the Kingdom of heaven has already been given to you.

Let's do a spiritual science experiment to help us learn how the laws of the Spirit work. Over the next seven days, explore how the Kingdom of God operates for yourself by learning to walk "according to the Spirit" even more (Romans 8:4). Think of one spiritual law you would like to explore and experience. You can revisit the preceding "Renew Your Mind" section, where you wrote down some spiritual laws, and pick one of your answers there. Or you can pick another spiritual law of your choosing. (For example, "give, and it will be given to you.") The Kingdom of God is vast, and the possibilities are endless. Write down the law you are choosing for this experiment:

_____

_____

If you chose the spiritual law "give, and it will be given to you," for example, over the next seven days you will see opportunities come your way to give abundantly. Stay present with the Holy Spirit as He teaches you about your chosen law. He will highlight unseen details about it for you, and He will give you wisdom as you act on that law physically. But you don't have to stop at experiencing the workings of one spiritual law. You will learn a lot about the heart and mind of God as you lean into SQ and go on to explore more of the different spiritual laws He has set in place.

*Revisit the *New Neural Pathfinder* tool now to track the spiritual progress you made throughout this lesson.

There are so many dimensions to SQ, which means there is so much water just waiting to be walked on, and so much of nature longing for a transcended experience with God. Literally, the natural world is coaxing us out of the boat of boring living and imploring us to discover the secrets of the universe.

Access God's Thoughts and Ideas

Maybe you've noticed that Christians can have a terrible fear of thinking. In my mind, our problem is twofold—rooted both in the way we view the Bible and in our deep-seated fear of deception. Let's look at each of these challenges a little more closely.

Problem number 1—the way we view the Bible

For many Christians, the Scriptures are a box, a limitation and a strong boundary embodying *all truth*. Their basic Christian belief is that if it's not in the Bible, it's (for the most part) not true. Yet nearly all Christians believe in things like air conditioning, modern transportation, electronic devices—tangible things that seem amoral (without moral value). These Christians' purchases are rarely affected by who invented, manufactured or distributed any product. Such believers are fine with enjoying inventions and/or innovations created by cultists, atheists or immoral activists, as long as you ignore the who behind the what. In the Christian community, positively acknowledging an unbeliever who may be behind innovative ideas can get you labeled as deceived, since the common culture of Christianity is guilt by association. This mindset creates a ton of anxiety, which ultimately robs people of creativity and derails invention and innovation.

Here are some questions to ponder: What if we viewed the Bible as an empowering platform instead of as a limiting container? What if we viewed God as bigger than His book?

I certainly am not talking about preaching a different gospel, or saying that there are many ways to God, or that there is no hell, or anything remotely similar to that. Nor am I suggesting that there are other Scriptures outside the 66 books of the Bible. Furthermore, I agree that we should never embrace any idea that is anti-biblical or anti-God. I am simply pointing out that the goal of the Bible is for us to get to know God. Furthermore, the entire Bible is true, but not everything that is true is in the Bible. For example, God created the principles of electricity and the laws of physics, but He did not explain them in the Scriptures. Yet understanding these laws and principles is the foundation for all modern invention and innovation.

We have been learning, however, that the Creator is revealed in all His creation. God is the originator of creativity, innovation and invention, and I'd like to suggest that although some of the greatest innovators and inventors were unbelievers, they thought like God—in that they had faith for the impossible. I call people like this unbelieving believers! We must understand that unbelievers do not have the power to take glory away from God; their creativity only reveals Him even more. Just because you don't believe in your Creator doesn't mean He doesn't believe in you, or isn't working through you.

Problem number 2—our deep-seated fear of being deceived

The second challenge many Christians face that destroys high levels of thinking is their deep-seated fear of being deceived. These fears are not completely irrational or unfounded. There are some very good reasons to be concerned about deception. Christian history is riddled with the dead spiritual bones of radical believers who went off to Hollywood, universities or some other place of "higher learning," only to return as liberal critics of the Kingdom.

Christians often have more faith in the devil's ability to deceive them than they have faith in the Holy Spirit's ability to lead them. But here is a question to ponder: What would happen if believers wholeheartedly placed their trust in the Holy Spirit to convict, counsel and comfort them when they are exploring un-traversed territory?

We must realize that creative thinking is in our DNA, and it is therefore part of God's nature in every believer. It is also important to understand that the culture of our community is equally important. It can either combat deception, or it can stifle our innovative nature to do what the Spirit has anointed us to do. In chapter 12 of *Spiritual Intelligence*, I talk about the importance of submitting to a culture that cultivates healthy character while also inspiring spiritual intelligence. All believers need the balance of having a community that both cares about an individual's relationship with God and sound doctrine, and encourages the pursuit of revelation, invention, innovation and creativity.

Remember, courageous people are not fearless; rather, they are people who refuse to let fear tell them what to do. God is guiding you out of bondage and into freedom. Complete the following exercises to help you conquer fear.

1. Recognize that fear is not from God. Read 1 John 4:18 and write down what perfect love does to fear.

2. Remember one of the weapons of your warfare—your testimony! In three or four sentences, write out a testimony that will help you recall that fear has no place in your walk with God.

> ### COGNITIVE CONNECTION
>
> Do you have a generalized fear of being deceived? If your answer is yes, where do you think this fear originated?

3. Remember that 2 Timothy 1:7 says you have been given a sound mind: "For God has not given us a spirit of fear, but of power and of love and of a sound mind" (NKJV). Record what this verse says about the things God has and has not given us. Where does fear fit in?

Renew Your Mind

Did you know that there is no such thing as laymen in the Kingdom of God; there is only a royal priesthood? All believers are therefore priests. What does this mean when it comes to creativity, innovation and invention? Can a "priest" be an innovator, a painter or a mechanic? We may be able to see the obvious ministry involved in parenting, preaching and teaching, but can ministry look like engineering, designing, developing or even discovering? I believe that it absolutely can. In fact, I know it does!

Do you believe fear and/or a religious mindset could have prevented you from pursuing a path of innovation, creativity or invention? Or have they derailed any other out-of-the-box pursuit, whatever that may look like? Perhaps fear has even caused you to devalue the work you are in now. Briefly explain how fear may be affecting you in any of these ways.

_____

_____

_____

_____

Read 1 Peter 2:9. In your own words, what does being a part of a "royal priesthood" mean to you? How do you see your role in this priesthood practically playing out on earth?

_____

_____

_____

_____

Romans 12:1 says, "Therefore I urge you, brethren, by the mercies of God, to present your bodies a living and holy sacrifice, acceptable to God, which is your spiritual service of worship." Write how you would define your "spiritual service of worship." (If you don't know, this would be an opportunity to invite the Holy Spirit to give you personalized insight into the vast possibilities of what this could look like in your life.)

_____

_____

_____

Build New Neural Pathways

Take some time with the Holy Spirit to discuss your responses to the questions above. What insights did you discover? Write them down.

_____

_____

_____

_____

_____

Are there opportunities that you could take, but you are hesitating because you feel it's too late? Have you been missing the ministry that is right in front of you, no matter the seeming importance (or seeming unimportance) of your occupation? As you process forward with the Holy Spirit, He will pull you out of the fog and into the light. He will convict your heart and restore your hope. I encourage you to tether yourself to the Holy Spirit and trust the discovery process.

*Revisit the *New Neural Pathfinder* tool now to track the spiritual progress you made throughout this lesson.

Engagement Tool

The Top 4

List the top 4 spiritual insights you gained from this module, whether they came from the thoughts in the lessons, the *Cognitive Connection* exercises, the "Renew Your Mind" reflections or the "Build New Neural Pathways" activations.

1. _____

_____

_____

_____

2. _____

_____

_____

_____

3. _____

_____

_____

_____

4. _____

_____

_____

Plan of Action

Create one action step based on the spiritual insights listed above that would demonstrate spiritual intelligence when you apply it to your daily life. Note that a good action step has a *who*, *what*, *how* and *when*. For example, if one of my takeaways from this module is that condemnation and the law of sin and death have been conquered through the law of the Spirit, I might create an action step like this: "At any given moment (*when*) that I am experiencing the presence of fear, condemnation or anxiety (*what*), I (*who*) will seek counsel from the Holy Spirit swiftly (*how*), since it is walking with the Spirit that gives me power, love and a sound mind."

*Note that the *Spiritual Intelligence Quotient (SQ) Assessment* in my SQ book will give you many other specific action steps you can take to further develop, deepen and implement your SQ, based on your score once you take the test.

Module 5

What Time Is It?

The Magi were stargazers who brought gifts to Jesus after His birth. Their lineage is traced all the way back to Daniel in Babylon. In fact, they were the spiritual grandsons of the prophet Daniel, who became chief of the magicians in the days of King Nebuchadnezzar. Daniel unseated the sorcerers of his day, as he was ten times wiser than all of them. Furthermore, he became the mentor of many of the magicians who turned to Jehovah from demons and idols. Even more inspiring is that the Magi inherited these spiritual skills and mastered discerning the divine spiritual season for what God had set in motion.

God is restoring our spiritual legacy by reviving within us the extraordinary faith of the mothers and fathers who preceded us in it. He is once again moving among His people with supernatural power and divine wisdom, and He is empowering us to be on time and in real time with Him. He is enlightening us to the realities of our spiritual inheritance and inviting us to change the course of history, as those who went before us once did.

Is there an ancestor of old in your family lineage or a historical figure of the faith you have always been very drawn to? For example, one of my great heroes in life is Abraham Lincoln—a history maker who will forever be known for his relentless pursuit to become the man he envisioned he could be, despite experiencing punishing failure, repeated defeat and an ongoing battle with depression. His legacy is a testimony of a practical life led by unwavering faith, unyielding hope and unstoppable love for those outside himself. Write one or more such names here:

_____

_____

What is it about your heroes of old that inspires you to think bigger and expand your possibilities?

_____

_____

_____

What spiritual gifting or spiritual intelligence do you believe these people functioned in?

_____

_____

If you could operate in their gifting, what do you imagine your life would be like? How do you think it would impact your family, your community or the world?

_____

_____

_____

_____

Trust that God knows the desires of your heart. He values the very people you do, likely for similar reasons and beyond. He values those who trust Him and step out in faith, and you are one of them! God is opening up new opportunities for you to grow in your supernatural abilities, because whether you believe it yet or are just beginning to believe it, you are an inspiration to someone. Your faith will be marked in history.

*For additional insights into module 5, read chapters 14–16 of my book *Spiritual Intelligence*.

Religious leaders of old were keenly aware that God creates "signs" that clearly communicate what are called "kairos" circumstances dictating the attitudes, mindsets and actions necessary to navigate His sovereign seasons successfully. Yet many spiritual leaders of our day are unable to "discern the signs of the time." Many believers are like ships without a compass, trying desperately to navigate the seas of humanity, yet unable to sail accurately and securely. Many don't know how to navigate the planning and preparation for such divine kairos times successfully.

Access God's Thoughts and Ideas

The ancient Greeks had two words for *time—chronos* and *kairos*. The Greek word *chronos* is where we get our English word *chronological*, referring to a clock or calendar. *Chronos* is used 54 times in the New Testament, and it is time that can be measured in seconds, minutes, hours and years.

The Greek word *kairos* is used 86 times in the New Testament, and it is qualitative. It measures moments, the right moment, the opportune moment, the perfect moment. It is important to know that the Greek word *kairos* in itself does not mean a divine time; it only describes a difference in the way we view time.

With that said, there are Kingdom kairos epochs—a period of time in history or in a person's life, notably marked by specific events or particular characteristics—that are predicated by a God-theme. These are kairos moments with a divine purpose and a presupposed outcome. They are moments when *divine favor meets divine opportunity*. They are often the result of the sovereignty of God transcending the free will of man.

I discuss this in more depth in chapter 14 of *Spiritual Intelligence*, but here it will be beneficial to list three things that often mark divine kairos epochs:

1. *Acceleration*—things that would normally take years happen suddenly (see the rebuilding of Jerusalem's walls in Nehemiah 1–6).

2. *Unusual occurrences*—things happen that seem outside the nature of God or unusual for the epoch season (see the story of Ananias and Sapphira in Acts 5:1–11).

3. *Supernatural interventions*—things that never happen suddenly occur against ridiculous odds (see the way the sun and moon stood still in Joshua 10:12–13).

We all live day in and day out in chronos conditions, planning around our calendar and staying in tune with time. Then, sometimes without warning, we get drawn into the vortex of eternity and experience the effects of infinity. These are the divine kairos times in history when God overrides our free will and creates a supernatural exception to the rule. He defies the laws of physics or interrupts the trajectory of natural history to impose His sovereign will over humankind.

As we know, history is primarily molded by the will of people—until it isn't. In other words, there are moments in time when God interrupts history and creates *His-story*. At those times, free will gives way to sovereignty, and chronos time yields to divine kairos moments.

The challenge is that if we are spiritually ignorant and are unaware of the "change in weather" (which I call divine kairos conditions), then we can end up like Balaam, who demonstrated that a smart jackass is better than a dumb prophet (see Numbers 22:21–35).

As I discussed in chapter 14 of my book, when we settle into trusting the Spirit to guide our lives and we begin to plug into our prophetic gifts, we can sometimes find ourselves living *in* the future instead of *from* the future. We need to honor the past, live in the present and look to the future. One challenge for prophetic people is that as they get insights into the future, they often begin to live there before it is actually available to them.

If this is you, I want to encourage you that I know all too well how sometimes a prophetic promise seems to take forever to be fulfilled. All the same, we must contend for the promise that tarries.

On the other hand, I have also observed many people over the years who were caught snoozing at the wheel, completely unaware of the third-heaven realities in motion around them. The question then becomes, How do we become like those people in Jesus' day who were *kairos conductors*—able to understand the times and discern the appropriate action or attitude necessary to find synergy for their divine seasons?

To accomplish this, one of the first questions we have to answer is, *Do we actually know what time it is?* We have to press into the Spirit to discern the times, the divine kairos moments in our epoch history. As we use our SQ expressed through the divine wisdom of the Spirit, I believe God is restoring our ability to understand the proper response to what is our epoch season.

Do you feel the Holy Spirit transitioning you into something new? Sometimes the greatest challenge we have in a new season is that we know too much about our previous mandate. We often resist what God is bringing us into, because many times we feel terribly disqualified and ill-equipped for a place we have never been before. In what ways have you found yourself resisting divine kairos moments?

> **COGNITIVE CONNECTION**
>
> Do you have a prophetic word or a calling on your life that has yet to be fulfilled? Describe it here:

If we resist kairos moments, it is no wonder that we then feel bored to death and disconnected from the Spirit. It is imperative in kairos transitions that we remain teachable and hungry so that we learn and grow. If you are battling with any sense of guilt,

COGNITIVE CONNECTION

Can you discern the spiritual season you are in currently? To help you put language to it, reference Solomon's list of seasons in Ecclesiastes 3:1–8. For example, Ecclesiastes 3:3 says there is "a time to tear down and a time to build up." If I sensed that I was in a season of preparing and building something new, I would write "I am in a building season" and describe how I know that is the case.

dread or fear when it comes to walking in Kingdom time with God, then set aside time to pray and ask the Holy Spirit to uncover anything that may be preventing you from stepping in time with God. Write whatever you hear.

Now ask Him how you can drop any resistance and welcome the new season He may be ushering into your life. Again, write whatever you hear.

Renew Your Mind

Referencing Solomon's list in Ecclesiastes 3 once again, let's say it is a time for peace, but you think it is a time for war. Instead of resting, you are found fighting. When this happens, you can miss out on the opportunities that God has placed amid each season. Have you ever struggled with a sense that you missed out on what God had for you at some point because you misunderstood the season you were in? Describe that experience:

_____

_____

_____

_____

_____

_____

_____

_____

God is giving you and me the grace to develop into spiritually intelligent kairos conductors. As you navigate through transitions, processes and change, the Holy Spirit will guide you, if you are willing to go forward with Him. Trust me, there is no better navigator than the Holy Spirit and no better place to be than in God's will. One thing I know for sure: Your calling and assignments throughout life may change, but who you are to God never will!

Build New Neural Pathways

Start viewing yourself as a kairos conductor. You were made to discern the signs of the times and to work with God, not ahead of Him or behind Him. The Holy Spirit will teach you how to recognize the signs of the times. One practical way to start training yourself to do this is to step back and discern what season you are in now. God will often use the challenges of our lives to inspire divine opportunities and open our spirits to new possibilities. Let's look at a current challenge you are facing and discern if there are divine opportunities in the midst of this season. Describe your current challenge:

_____

_____

Some people see a problem in every opportunity, but great people see an opportunity in every problem. What divine opportunity do you see in the midst of your struggle? Ask the Holy Spirit to uncover anything you may not recognize or may even be resisting.

_____

_____

Ask the Holy Spirit what action steps you need to take to move forward in this divine opportunity.

_____

_____

Share what you have uncovered with the people you named earlier whom you invited to join you on this journey. Pray over this section together and be sure to share any movement, insights or affirmation that you get along the way as you develop into a child of God who walks in time with the living God.

* *

*Revisit the *New Neural Pathfinder* tool now to track the spiritual progress you made throughout this lesson.

Lesson 2—The Spiritual Internet

The Greeks could not envision a God who lives outside the laws of physics and who is omnipresent everywhere at once, working through different gifts and various people all at the same time. It is important that we remember that God is not human; He is *God*.

Access God's Thoughts and Ideas

The apostle Paul had his work cut out for him when he set out to teach the Corinthians, who were former polytheists (meaning they believed in multiple gods), how the spirit world actually worked. They were moving in the gifts of the Holy Spirit but were having a hard time reconciling with the fact that each gift of the Spirit was not a different god. They had superimposed their doctrine of polytheism over their experience. In other words, they were having the right experience but holding to the wrong theology. It is why in 1 Corinthians 12:1–11 Paul repeatedly uses the word *same*—*same* Spirit, *same* Lord, *same* God (emphasis added). He was driving home that there is only one God:

> Now concerning spiritual gifts, brethren, I do not want you to be unaware. You know that when you were pagans, you were led astray to the mute idols, however you were led. . . .
>
> Now there are varieties of gifts, but the *same* Spirit. And there are varieties of ministries, and the *same* Lord. There are varieties of effects, but the *same* God who works all things in all persons. But to each one is given the manifestation of the Spirit for the common good. For to one is given the word of wisdom through the Spirit, and to another the word of knowledge according to the *same* Spirit; to another faith by the *same* Spirit, and to another gifts of healing by the *one* Spirit, and to another the effecting of miracles, and to another prophecy, and to another the distinguishing of spirits, to another various kinds of tongues, and to another the interpretation of tongues. But one and the *same* Spirit works all these things, distributing to each one individually just as He wills.

Notice also that Paul described manifestations of the Holy Spirit as *gifts*, *ministries* and *effects* (see verses 4–6).

- The word *gifts* is the Greek word *charisma*, and in this passage it means "spiritual abilities." These are all actually different dimensions of spiritual intelligence and supernatural power.
- The word *ministry* in this passage is the Greek word *diakonia*, which means "spiritual occupations." This could refer to a teacher, pastor, evangelist and so forth.
- The word *effect* is the Greek word *energeo*. It means "spiritual accomplishments," as in work achieved or performed by the Spirit, such as when a person is saved by the direction of the Spirit, or when the Holy Spirit flowing through a believer heals a marriage.

COGNITIVE CONNECTION

Have you ever noticed how a spiritual gift, ministry or effect can manifest differently through various people or have different manifestations in diverse environments? For example, a word of knowledge can be used to diagnose a health issue in a person's life, or to troubleshoot an automobile's problem through an automotive technician's ministry (as would happen in my case when I owned my auto parts and repair shops). Can you recall a time when you personally experienced or witnessed some of the variety of ways in which the gifts can work?

---

*See more about this in chapter 16 of my book, where I also provide a brief overview and definition of some of the Holy Spirit's gifts to us.

I would like to point out a few various manifestations that are almost like having a spiritual Internet in operation. In fact, that is indeed how they work.

1. *AirDropping* is a spiritual dynamic that takes place as a result of the Holy Spirit living in us individually and collectively at the same time. This gives us a spiritual connection in that our *human* spirits are in union with one another through the conduit of the Holy Spirit. We can "AirDrop" spiritual gifts to one another by way of the Holy Spirit. Paul reminded his disciple Timothy of the AirDrop that took place in his spirit, urging him to make progress with the spiritual gift that was bestowed to him through prophetic words and the laying on of hands (see 1 Timothy 4:14–15; also see more about this and the next two manifestations in chapter 16 of *Spiritual Intelligence*).

2. *Spiritual collective reasoning* is in operation when each of us has a piece of the truth, but collectively we have the mind of Christ. The apostle Paul wrote in 1 Corinthians 2:16 that "we have the mind of Christ," the operative word here being *we*. Romans 12:4–5 teaches that "just as we have many members in one body and all the members do not have the same function, so we, who are many, are one body in Christ, and individually members one of another." In other words, spiritual collective intelligence is a manifestation of the Spirit flowing in harmony through individual members of the Body of Christ.

3. *Spiritual inheritance* is a dimension of spiritual intelligence that is profound but often overlooked. It is personified in 2 Timothy 1:5: "For I am mindful of the sincere faith within you [Timothy], which first dwelt in your grandmother Lois and your mother Eunice, and I am sure that it is in you as well." The Bible strongly implies that Timothy's faith was the result of a spiritual inheritance from his grandmother and mother. The spirit world transcends time and space. When someone wins a personal victory with God, it therefore becomes a potential

---

COGNITIVE CONNECTION

Can you recall a time when you personally experienced the impartation of a spiritual gift? What gift did you feel was imparted to you? List three ways you could further develop that gift in your life.

---

spiritual inheritance to those who come after that person in the Spirit.

Renew Your Mind

Writer and futurist Alvin Toffler made a profound statement that is a powerful warning for us all: "The illiterate of the future will not be the person who cannot read. It will be the person who does not know how to learn." Often, when it comes to the spiritual gifts, ministries or effects that we just talked about, believers can become so steeped in religion, jealousy and offense that they literally forget how to learn. We must refuse to allow the work of the enemy to stunt us spiritually and disconnect us from everything inside the Kingdom of God.

Take time with the Holy Spirit and ask Him to show you what you are developing in with excellence spiritually. Also ask the Spirit to highlight any sort of a religious mindset, or areas of offense or jealousy that may be shutting down your growth in SQ. Use this space to record your time with the Holy Spirit.

Build New Neural Pathways

Do you walk in spiritual gifts that people often recognize in you and wish they had? Or vice-versa, is there someone in your every-day life whom you admire, whose walk with the Lord is inspiring to you? Write the name of the person you admire here:

_____

I encourage you to share with this person what you have learned in this study about "AirDropping" in the Spirit. Get together with this person and/or with other believers and lay hands on one another to release gifts to one another. Then begin to step out in faith and exercise the gift you have been desiring. As you see it manifest in your life, share the testimony with others, and eagerly encourage one another to develop the gifts you have received.

*Revisit the *New Neural Pathfinder* tool now to track the spiritual progress you made throughout this lesson.

Many of the Old Testament believers were world changers! I mean, wouldn't you love for your name even to be whispered among those in the hall of faith—saints like Abraham, Sarah, Moses, Joshua or even King David, the man after God's heart? Or how about the great prophets Elijah, Elisha and Deborah, men and women who literally shifted the course of nations? Yet the truth is that if you are a born-again believer, you have an incredible advantage over any of the Old Testament saints.

Access God's Thoughts and Ideas

The Old Testament was the dispensation before Jesus came. When He died on the cross, Scripture says that we died with Him, and when He rose again, we rose with Him (see Romans 6). It also says, "Therefore if anyone is in Christ, he is a new creature; the old things passed away; behold, new things have come" (2 Corinthians 5:17). The word *new* here is the Greek word *kainos*, which can be translated as "prototype"—something never before created. When we received Christ, we became creatures who had never before graced this planet. Consequently, the blood of Jesus didn't just cleanse us from all sin; it transformed us into the likeness of Christ. In fact, the Bible says, "Therefore be imitators of God, as beloved children" (Ephesians 5:1). The goal of discipleship through a life in the Spirit is to become like God. Notice that I did not say we are to become a god! I'm simply pointing out that in Christ we are a new "prototype," discerning, learning and maturing in His ways. That is fascinating to me!

God empowered us to do greater works than Christ did, so we can ascertain that being Christlike is more than having a noble character; it is also operating in divine power. Let me count the ways that we have been supernaturally equipped even more than our Old Testament counterparts. (You can see this list in even greater detail in chapter 16 of my book.)

COGNITIVE CONNECTION

Describe yourself as a "prototype" of God's amazing creation:

_____

_____

_____

_____

_____

_____

_____

_____

_____

_____

_____

1. *We are born-again.* We have a new heart and a new mind (see Ezekiel 36:26; 1 Corinthians 2:16). Old Testament believers had a sin nature, but we are saints, meaning "holy believers."

2. *We are seated in heavenly places with Christ.* Our heavenly seat gives us eternal perspectives (see Ephesians 2:6; Revelation 4:1), whereas non-Christians are relegated only to the first heaven.

3. *The Creator Himself actually lives inside us* (see 1 Corinthians 3:16). In the Old Testament, the Spirit came *on* people, but in the New Testament, He lives *in* us.

4. *We are friends with God* (see John 15:15). Friendship with God releases divine revelation in us.

5. *We have angelic insights and angel oversight* (see Acts 10:3–7; Hebrews 1:5–14).

6. *We have been enlightened as believers* (see Hebrews 6:4).

7. *We have access to the powers of the age to come* (see Hebrews 6:5).

8. *We can't fail!* Our divine advantage is that God prepared our work before He created us in Christ, so we are destined to win (see Ephesians 2:10). This is all "in Christ," meaning that those without Christ have yet to experience this divine benefit.

9. *We have been given authority and power over all the power of the evil one* (see Luke 9:1). Pre-Christians are under the power and influence of the devil (see Ephesians 2:1–2).

10. *We have been given all authority to make disciples of all nations* (see Matthew 28:18–20). Believers are specifically called to lead nations and be cultural architects.

11. *We have at least five dimensions of wisdom, the first dimension* being that we have the Holy Spirit's gift of wisdom (see 1 Corinthians 12:8).

12. *The second dimension* is that we have the wisdom rooted in the mind of Christ (see 1 Corinthians 2:16).

13. *The third dimension* is that we have the timeless wisdom founded in eternity, called "the wisdom from the age to come" (see 1 Corinthians 2:6–7).

14. *The fourth dimension* is that we have the "manifold wisdom of God," which is multidimensional (see Ephesians 3:10).

15. *The fifth dimension* is that we have the collective wisdom rooted in impartation and cooperative reasoning (see Romans 1:11).

16. *We have the gift of prophecy*, which can happen in these ways:
    • Foretelling—the ability to know the future before it happens
    • Forthtelling—causing the future with God's prophetic insights (see 1 Corinthians 12:10; Ezekiel 37:1–10)

17. *We have the gift of discernment.* This helps us navigate the unseen realm holistically (see 1 Corinthians 12:10; 1 John 4:1–4).

18. *We have the Holy Spirit in us*, who guides us "into *all* the truth" (John 16:13, emphasis added).

19. *We have the Spirit of revelation resting on us*, who gives us insights into the Word of God (see Ephesians 1:17).

20. *We have the gift of the word of knowledge*, by which we know facts through the insights of the Holy Spirit (see 1 Corinthians 12:8).

As modern-day believers, we often are not triumphant because the wisdom we get from God is imprisoned in us, and it is guarded by the spirit of religion, shackled for generations by the fear of man, and locked away by mediocrity that undermines excellence

COGNITIVE CONNECTION

If the list you just read is true about believers, and if we are at an even greater advantage than the Old Testament heroes of the faith, what would it look like for us as Christians to be leading in every realm of society in our day?

and kills inspiration. If we truly understood our advantages in the way we have been supernaturally equipped, think about the difference it would make in our lives and in the world around us.

Renew Your Mind

I asked at the beginning of this lesson if you would love for your name even to be whispered among those in the hall of faith. Yet the truth is that if you are a born-again believer, you have an incredible advantage over any of the Old Testament saints I mentioned. You just read the list of advantages we have. When you consider the truth that we have these advantages, what impossibilities now seem possible to you as a child of God?

It is often hard for us to experience our theology as a reality, simply because we try to process spiritual things (SQ) through a natural filter (IQ). Paul tells us in 1 Corinthians 2:14 that it is not possible to understand things of the Spirit with a natural mind. In order for us to take hold of the divine advantages we have in Christ, we must therefore tap into spiritual intelligence. Take another look at the list of our advantages and record the ones you feel you have experienced personally.

Using your spiritual intelligence, ask the Holy Spirit to help you process any of the God-given advantages that you have not experienced from the list and why. Ask Him to show you how they can become part of what you experience in Christ. Identify those spiritual advantages that are still ahead for you and note them here:

Build New Neural Pathways

The Church is entering into a spiritual awakening that you are part of! What's more, God has given you angelic help (see number 5 in the list of our advantages). Angels are ministering spirits who have been assigned to us for some important reasons. They give us insight, informing us with accurate and supernatural understanding (see Acts 10:3–7). They also provide oversight, coming alongside us with care and supervision, to help us see things through (see Hebrews 1:5–14).

Have you ever had any sense that God has sent angels to inform you or to serve you, as described in the Scripture passages just cited? Describe the experience below that led you to believe that angels were involved in a situation.

---

*Revisit the *New Neural Pathfinder* tool now to track the spiritual progress you made throughout this lesson.

Here is one of King Solomon's wise insights into the subject of inheritance: "A good man leaves an inheritance to his children's children, and the wealth of the sinner is stored up for the righteous" (Proverbs 13:22).

Access God's Thoughts and Ideas

Have you ever considered that the spiritual race you are running is not just for yourself? There are those who have gone before you—the great cloud of witnesses who are awaiting their reward, which is in you. They are a family of watching witnesses who are chronicling your profound narrative. The author of Hebrews uncovered this divine dynamic:

> Therefore, since we have so great a cloud of witnesses surrounding us, let us also lay aside every encumbrance and the sin which so easily entangles us, and let us run with endurance the race that is set before us, fixing our eyes on Jesus, the author and perfecter of faith, who for the joy set before Him endured the cross, despising the shame, and has sat down at the right hand of the throne of God.
>
> Hebrews 12:1–2

The Greek word *cloud* in this passage is *nephos*, meaning "a mass of clouds." A cloud of heavenly hosts has amassed to bear witness to your race, to watch your fight and to record your epic exploits! Just imagine the "who's who" of the faith, the celebrities of heaven, the true heroes of God, standing to their feet and cheering you on as you run the race that has been set before you.

You should also know that the race set before you is for those who are with you presently, who benefit from your relationship with Jesus, as well as for those who are yet to be born. The truth is that our level of spiritual intelligence not only honors those who have gone before us, but will determine the impact we have on

> **COGNITIVE CONNECTION**
>
> Among that cloud of witnesses, whom do you expect to greet on your homecoming?
>
> _____
>
> _____
>
> _____
>
> _____

those who will inherit the future. The more we experience transcended thinking—thinking beyond the confines of time and space, and thinking beyond the limits of human reasoning—the greater impact it will have on the legacy we leave for the generations to come.

As believers press into the mind of Christ and learn to think like God, there will be an epic rising of men, women and children of every age and ethnicity who are filled with inspired revelations, insights and supernatural solutions. God's people will shine the divine light of His wisdom brightly for all the world to see. This light will never be extinguished; it will not grow dim. It will be passed on from generation to generation, from glory to ever-increasing glory, and the cloud of witnesses who are watching from above will cheer us on all the way to the finish line.

> **COGNITIVE CONNECTION**
>
> Consider those who will be birthed into your inheritance, who will one day stand on your shoulders as you become a part of their great cloud of witnesses. What are you doing today to empower those people who have yet to be born?
>
> _____
>
> _____
>
> _____
>
> _____
>
> _____
>
> _____

Renew Your Mind

It is so important that we find our place of calling in life, and that we understand that each of us is born to be an instrument of God, filled with the Spirit of God, to do the works of God. You were made to experience spiritual intelligence on a level that has never occurred in the history of the world. This might be hard to grasp, but you are one of God's solutionaries on the earth!

Describe in your own words what being God's solutionary might look like for you. Be as clear, concise and vivid as possible. Here are a few questions to help you engage your divine imagination along these lines:

If you could not fail at it, what human problem would you feel called to solve?

_____

_____

_____

How would solving this problem impact the world spiritually, morally, sociologically, economically or even technologically?

_____

_____

_____

_____

_____

What would your team look like, and where would you be positioned geographically?

_____

_____

_____

_____

_____

What divine favor and supernatural resources do you imagine that you, as God's solutionary, might need?

_____

_____

_____

_____

_____

Build New Neural Pathways

As you have worked through this manual, maybe you have noticed that a divine shift is taking place in your spirit. Like the instinctive nature in birds that migrate south in the winter, you are experiencing a spiritual awakening and are making the voyage back to your Creator, Lover and Friend. As your SQ is increasing, new neural pathways are being bulldozed beyond any doubts, fears and lower-level thinking.

To live a life that goes beyond your humanness and reflects your identity as God's spiritually intelligent child, I encourage you to write out a one-hundred-year vision. It might feel overwhelming to think through, but you could start by revisiting your response in the previous "Renew Your Mind" exercise. Envision the solution you described extending beyond your lifetime. Spend time with God, dream with Him and write this vision together. Meditate on His Word, and as vision comes, write it down. You do not have to do this all in one sitting, but the time is now to begin building a legacy that will change the course of history.

As you begin that process, I will leave you with this final declaration: May our children's children's children say of us, "That generation truly had the mind of Christ; they were the pioneers of spiritual intelligence who paved the way for our generation."

My One-Hundred-Year Vision

_____

_____

_____

_____

_____

_____

_____

_____

_____

_____

_____

_____

_____

_____

*Revisit the *New Neural Pathfinder* tool now to track the spiritual progress you made throughout this lesson.

Engagement Tool

The Top 4

List the top 4 spiritual insights you gained from this module, whether they came from the thoughts in the lessons, the *Cognitive Connection* exercises, the "Renew Your Mind" reflections or the "Build New Neural Pathways" activations.

1. _____

_____

_____

_____

2. _____

_____

_____

_____

3. _____

_____

_____

_____

4. _____

_____

_____

_____

Plan of Action

Create one action step based on the spiritual insights listed above that would demonstrate spiritual intelligence when you apply it to your daily life. Note that a good action step has a *who*, *what*, *how* and *when*. For example, if one of the supernatural solutions I learned from this module is that the Holy Spirit is empowering me as a believer to lead the sphere of influence God has given me, I would create an action step like this: "I (*who*) will actively take ownership of the role that I have in my family, community and career (*what*), leading in these areas of my influence with divine wisdom and supernatural solutions (*how*), starting today (*when*)."

_____

_____

_____

_____

_____

_____

_____

_____

_____

*Note that the *Spiritual Intelligence Quotient (SQ) Assessment* in my SQ book will give you many other specific action steps you can take to further develop, deepen and implement your SQ, based on your score once you take the test.

New Neural Pathfinder

a spiritual intelligence tracking tool

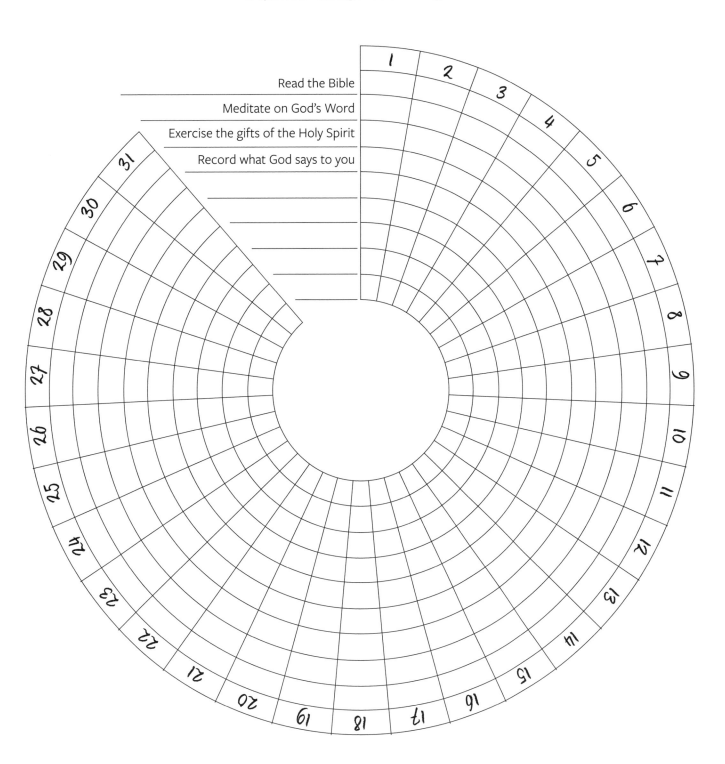

Read the Bible

Meditate on God's Word

Exercise the gifts of the Holy Spirit

Record what God says to you

New Neural Pathfinder

a spiritual intelligence tracking tool

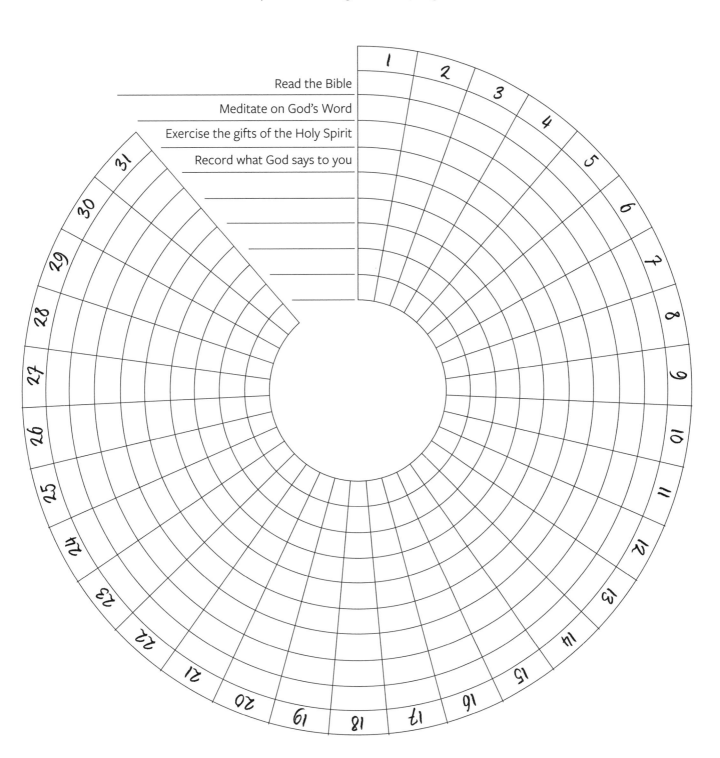

Read the Bible

Meditate on God's Word

Exercise the gifts of the Holy Spirit

Record what God says to you

New Neural Pathfinder

a spiritual intelligence tracking tool

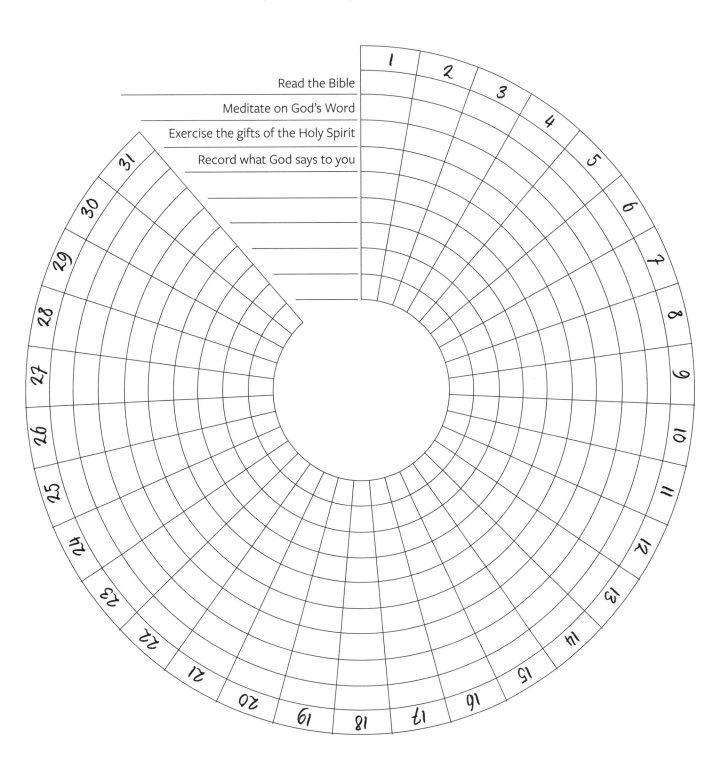

Read the Bible

Meditate on God's Word

Exercise the gifts of the Holy Spirit

Record what God says to you

New Neural Pathfinder

a spiritual intelligence tracking tool

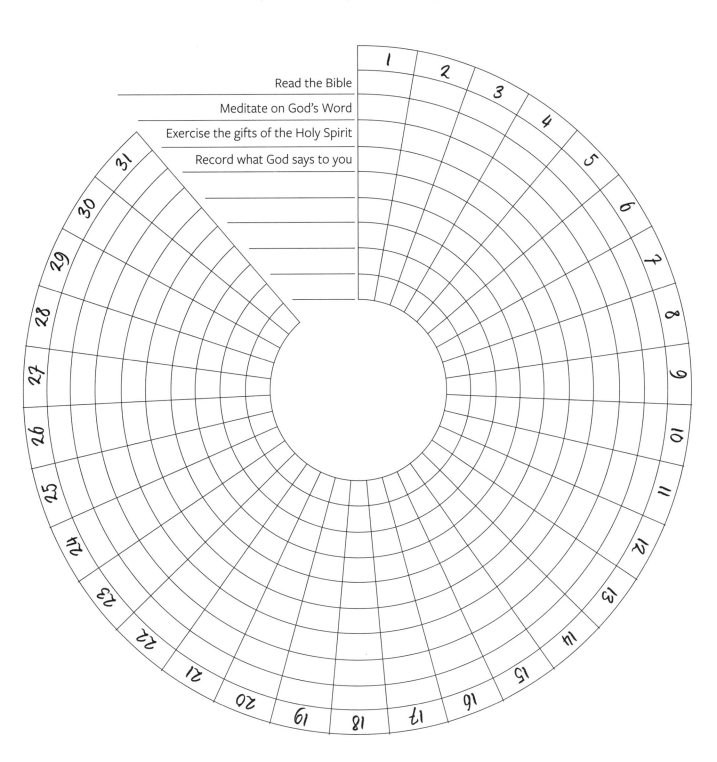

Read the Bible

Meditate on God's Word

Exercise the gifts of the Holy Spirit

Record what God says to you

New Neural Pathfinder

a spiritual intelligence tracking tool

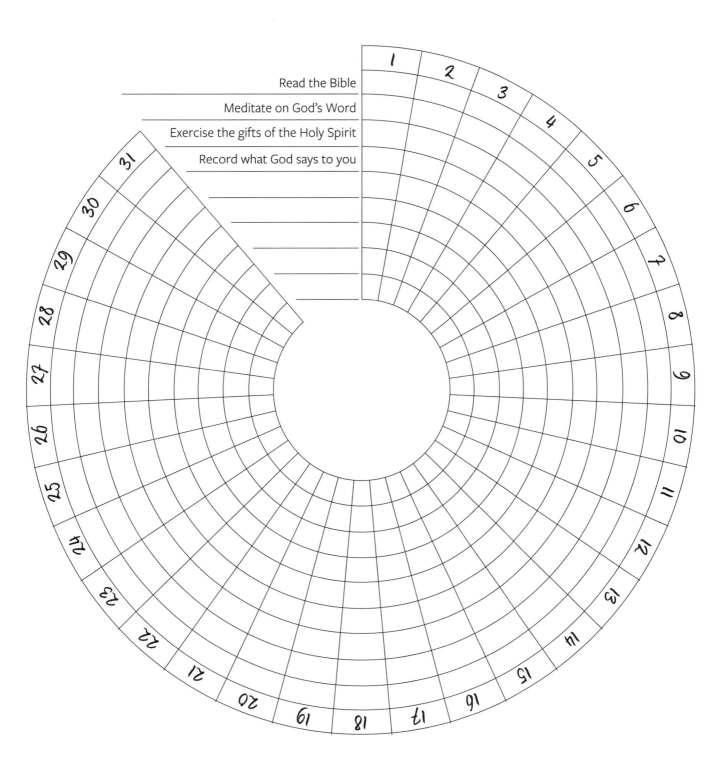

Read the Bible

Meditate on God's Word

Exercise the gifts of the Holy Spirit

Record what God says to you

New Neural Pathfinder

a spiritual intelligence tracking tool

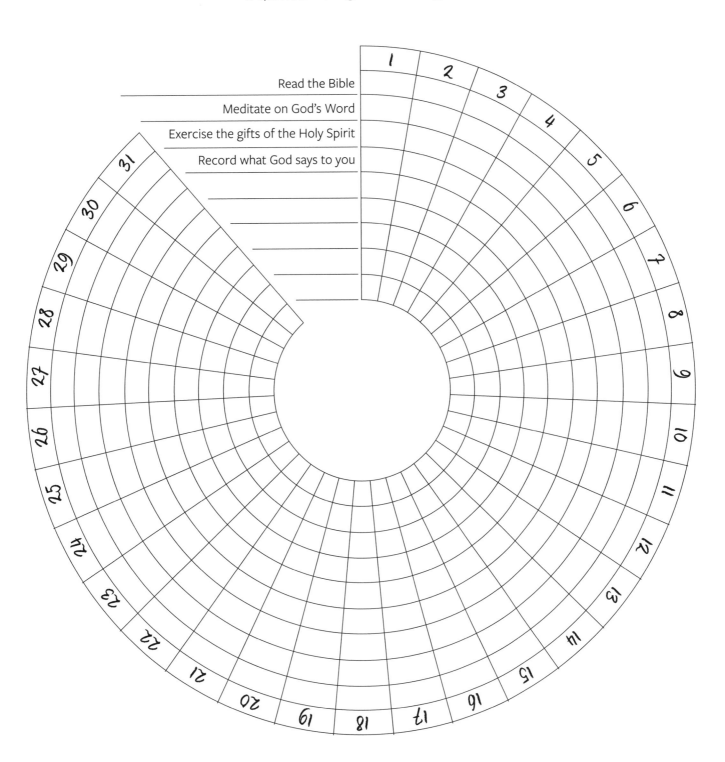

Read the Bible

Meditate on God's Word

Exercise the gifts of the Holy Spirit

Record what God says to you

New Neural Pathfinder

a spiritual intelligence tracking tool

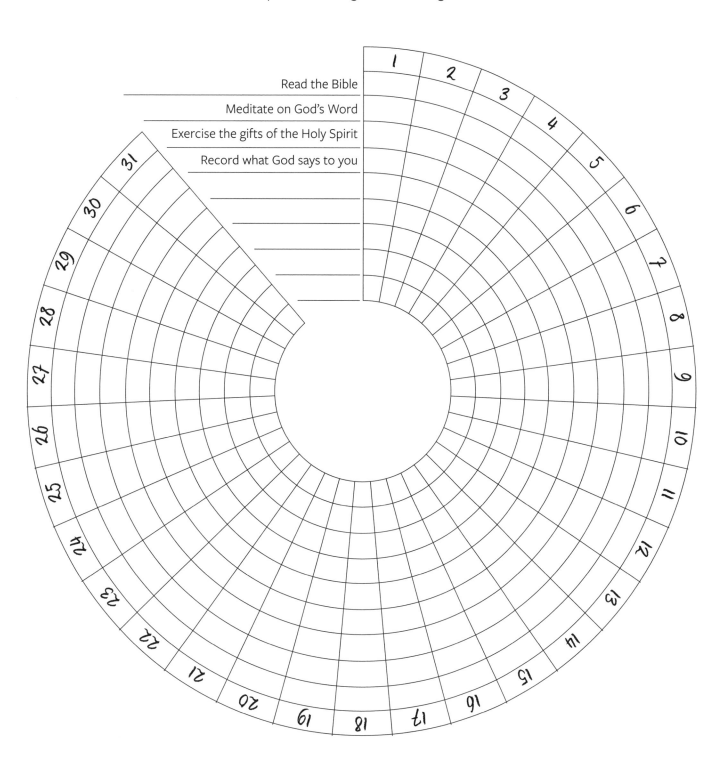

Read the Bible

Meditate on God's Word

Exercise the gifts of the Holy Spirit

Record what God says to you

Kris Vallotton is the senior associate leader of Bethel Church in Redding, California, and co-founder of Bethel School of Supernatural Ministry and Bethel Media. He is also the founder of Moral Revolution and Bethel School of Technology, as well as the chairman of Advance Redding. Kris is a bestselling author and has written more than a dozen books and manuals. He is also an international conference speaker and leadership consultant. He and his wife, Kathy, live in Redding and have four children and a growing number of grandchildren. Learn more at krisvallotton .com.

Spiritual Intelligence
Master Class

You Have the Mind of Christ
and the Spiritual Capacity for Brilliance

In the first Master Class of its kind, Kris Vallotton guides you through the reality of what it means to have the mind of Christ. This online course, designed to enhance your experience with *Basic Training for Spiritual Intelligence*, uses engaging teaching and interactive exercises that will develop your capacity for spiritual intelligence and bring to light God's life-transforming thoughts and ideas.

In this journey of discovery, you will

- learn how to build new neural pathways that will increase your spiritual capacity and open you to profound untapped potential
- gain keys to develop the biblical promise of a "renewed mind," including how to access God's thoughts and ideas, so you can bring heaven's solutions to life's challenges
- develop your spiritual aptitude with content that is structured and customized for interactive learning

Visit sqinstitute.com to learn more.